A Journey into Another World

Sojourn in Suriname

Terrence J. McCarthy, Sr.

A Journey into Another World: Sojourn in Suriname

Published by Wheatmark®
610 East Delano Street, Suite 104,
Tucson, Arizona 85705 U.S.A.
www.wheatmark.com

ISBN: 978-1-60494-424-2
LCCN: 2010927452

Dedication

My wife, Thecla, who has published two books,
10 Ambassadors to Costa Rica
and
My Liberated Life.
All 12 of my children.
My spiritual family, the Secular Franciscan Order.

Contents

Preface

In 1968 while working at Texas A&M University, Engineering Extension Service, the Aluminum Company of America (ALCOA) contacted the service for someone to train equipment operators and mechanics at their Suriname Operations.

This was the first time I was aware of the existence of a country called Suriname. Suriname can be spelled with an "e" at the end or not, I choose to use the "e". After a bit of research, some bells started to ring. Suriname turns out to be the former Dutch Guyana, located on the northeast coast of South America with the Atlantic Ocean to the north, French Guyana to the east, Brazil to the south and formerly British Guyana, presently Guiana, to the west.

In 1667 the British gave up Guiana for what is now New York while the Dutch gave up "New York" for Guiana. While this was a real swinging swap, no one seems to know just who the real winner was (is). At this time (1968), Suriname is a part of the Netherlands Empire, which consists of Holland, Suriname and the islands of the Greater Antilles, Aruba, Bonaire and Curazao (sometimes called the A, B, C, islands) off the coast of Venezuela.

The country of Suriname is often called the UN in miniature. The people and their well-preserved cultures make up a small but fantastic tapestry of togetherness. Any student of culture and/or history would do well to spend some time in this country.

Further investigation began to show an ever increasing number of things to explore. Stories of the Amazon valley with all the real wild and weird things to be found have intrigued me as they do most everyone else. It has always been a matter of curiosity for me to find some points of interest every place I have lived.

The ALCOA subsidiary in Suriname was SURALCO, SURiname ALuminum COmpany. Having an agreement with Alcoa, moving the family and settling in at Paramaribo, the capitol city, did not leave much time for thinking of the local culture. Once settled in there would be time to decide on a trip to the interior.

My wife, Thecla, and some of the children went to Costa Rica for their vacation.* My vacation was a trip into the interior of Suriname on the border of Brazil. Following is the planning for the trip and the journey

Suriname 55.142 sq. mi. Area
Population 400 to 450,000
Over 90% of the population live by the coast.
90% is essentially unpopulated

* Thecla McCarthy, My Liberated Life, Chapter V

MAP OF SURINAME

BRAZIL

By Terry McCarthy, Sr.

Note! Black dots denote locations

Acknowledgments

This is rather late to make acknowledgements for the help and advice on this Journey. The Journey was made in 1970 and this is being written in 2009. These were the people who helped me in the planning and executing on this undertaking. Many of them are deceased but they need to be recognized. With much gratitude and respect I submit them to you.

Robert McCarthy, my brother, who did a great job of going over the manuscript for me.

Fr. Donicie, a Dutch missionary
Mr. Peter Bolwerk, Surinam Museum
Mr. Claude Leavitt, Missionary
Mr. Neal Bittle, Missionary Aviation Fellowship
Mr. H. Coutinho, Suralco
Mr. J. Malm, Suralco Geological
Mr. J. Janssen, Suralco Moengo Operations
Mr. Rambharos, Suralco Mining
Mr. L. MacArthur, Suralco, Paranam Operations

1

Countdown and Departure

It would be difficult indeed to put my finger on how I decided where to go or why. From some years back, Brazil seemed a fascinating place to go. The plans began to take a general form of flying into the interior, walking about for a while then flying back. Depending on where I went, there was also the possibility of flying in and then back out by canoe. The actual route was not firmed up until about a week before departure.

The trip became: flying to Sipaliwini, the southern most airport in Suriname, almost due south of Paramaribo, have three Trio Indians from Alalapadu meet me there, walk to Pousoe Tirio Brazil, then to Alalapadu, Suriname. From there, walk to the head waters of the Tapanahoni River then by canoe down the Tapanahoni River to where the Paloemeu River joins it. This is where the town of Paloemeu is located (on the official Suriname map this is called Americankandre) and from there by plane back to Paramaribo. The time allowed was three weeks, leaving me one more week of vacation to rest up after the trip or allowing time for delays on the trip. The overall schedule worked out fine: however, the point to point schedule was off. The walking portion was about 160kms—straight line, the way we walked would be more.

As usual, one of the cheapest things in the world is advice.

Some people thought the idea was great, some were sure I was nuts (not a new idea) and others said that if anyone goes deep in the jungle they never come back. Some of these people had spent time doing various things deep in the interior, others had never been outside of town.

All were well-intentioned and they all added to the store of information needed. Being my own tour organizer etc., all information was welcomed. It was sometimes necessary to listen for long periods of time while the air was filled with words in order to pick up a small fragment of useful information. One example was the food requirements.

One man, who had spent a considerable amount of time in the interior on scientific and technical expeditions, gave me the following advice, in part: small can of sardines or beef per day, ½ cup of vegetable oil per day, soda biscuits (in tin), small cans of condensed milk, etc., etc. For someone on an unlimited budget and wishing to live in comfort, this would be a good deal. Another man, part Indian and part Negro, who was born and raised in a jungle village, told me to take only the very basics like salt, coffee, sugar, tea, and the likes. Other food would be provided by the Indians. They would need shotgun shells. It was such extremes that required some sort of reasonable calculations on what supplies would go. A complete list of the supplies taken is attached.

As with all such undertakings, there is the humor side that makes it all worth the effort. While all of the items needed were available in Suriname, it is a real challenge to find them. Locating a compass took the better part of a morning. At long last, a jewelry store had a line of fine quality compasses. Locating a snake bite kit was the real winner. My very good friend, Mr. Rambharos, a man I have learned to love and respect, knew what a snake bite kit was. We started looking for one by visiting everyplace we could imagine that may have one. Because of the language problems and that they are an almost unknown item, I made no attempt to ask about them. Ram did the asking and I did the looking. Leaving one store, Ram had a rather amused look on his face, and said, "after I asked for a snake bite kit, the girl asked 'why do you want to bite a snake'"? Later, by way of the company's geological department, a kit was purchased.

Here, as well as in most all other places, the only time anything moves is when one moves it himself. Each detail had to be worked out and then checked out. Slowly supplies built up, information began to firm up and the loose ends began to come together

Friday July 31, 1970.

My wife, Thecla, son Kevin and I stopped in to see Fr. Donicie, a local priest from Holland. Father had spent much time in the bush and was one of my prime sources of sound information. We talked about my plans to the interior and enjoyed a beer. At this time, the first priest from the local seminary, newly ordained, joined the conversation but not the beer. At last it was time to ask Father for his blessing. Fr. Donicie suggested that as long as the new Father was present he should give the blessing. The new priest was Waldie Wong Loi Sing, ordained on July 19th, made his priesthood just 12 days old. After all, being newly ordained, his blessing would have all that new innocence. Fr. Donicie felt that his many years in the priesthood may have given his blessing some tarnish. However, I felt that with his greater experience his would provide a more understanding blessing and the new Father more power so they both gave us their blessing and we left for home.

Fr. Donicie, a Dutchman, had spent most of his 35 plus years as a priest here in Suriname. He had worked with the U.S. servicemen here in W.W.II so knew English and the American way of doing things. He was known and respected by the Indians and the Bush Negroes as well as the people in the city. If Father did not have an answer, he sure knew who did. (The Bush Negroes were early slaves who revolted and went deep into the jungle to live as they had in Africa. They were sometimes called Djukas)

Saturday August 1.

Everything that was to be taken on the trip was at home except for a moetete. A moetete is the local version of the backpack. It is a basket woven by the Indians or Bush Negroes. The size and quality of the basket depends on its use. Basically, the basket is the same as any other rectangular basket. The moetete, however, is open at one end. The top end is open so the contents can extended out as required. The moetete is equipped with straps for the shoulders and one to go over the head. The straps are bark cut from a special tree—they are soft and pliable—for a few days.

We had been trying to get a moetete for some time but had not been successful. On the last day, it was necessary to reach over and touch the panic button. We asked a friend to ask a friend to ask a friend if we could borrow his moetete: late in the afternoon we had the moetete. Larry MacArthur and his grandmother came to show me how to pack.

Larry's grandmother was a full-blooded Indian who was the youngest 80 year old I ever met. She learned to speak English from the missionaries in her native village in the former British Guyana. Larry MacArthur is a native Surinamer, he had been in the Dutch Navy submarine service. His wife is from Holland. Larry is one of the men I am training to be an instructor of heavy equipment mechanics. We became good friends and hopefully I have been able to help him as much as he helped me.

We began by placing the large sheet of plastic inside the moetete, then all the items were packed in the moetete and the plastic folded over the entire contents. A nylon line was used to lace the basket opening together making it a very compact and watertight package.

With all of the gear and supplies packed, there remained only one thing to do: check out the airplane. One of my objectives while living here was to learn how to fly. There was an on again and off again Aero Club at the local airport of Zorg en Hoop. They had two airplanes, one Super Cub and a Cessna 182. I planned to use the 182 for the flight to Sipaliwini. It was now time to make sure the bird was still operational. The plane was ready except to top off the tanks. At the time, the fuel pump was inaccessible, so the men at the hangar agreed to top the tanks later in the afternoon.

At 7:00 p.m. the family went to Mass, which would allow me to leave early in the morning.

Sunday August 2.

Sleep was very evasive, nothing was bothering me, it just seemed that after getting everything pulled together, sleep was the least important thing. We were up at the usual 6:00 a.m. and started to make breakfast. At about 7:45 we were at the airport. The plane was outside the hangar; we unlocked it and put the moetete in the luggage compartment. Going over the pre-flight check, I found the tanks had not been topped off so we began looking for a key to the gas pump. No key could be found for the Aero Club's gas pump. After some frantic phone calls, we were able to get gas at the SLM (Suriname National Airlines, the local extension of KLM) pump.

Mr. Ed Kelly, a US expatriate with an ATR (Airline Transport Rating) rating, aero club instructor and a chief pilot for SLM, was the pilot in command: this was only the second time for me in the 182. Even though I was in the right seat, it gave me great cross-country experience. Kelly made out the flight plan: estimated air time to Sipaliwini, two hours and 55 minutes, fuel on board for nine hours (this 182 had long range tanks), true airspeed 100 knots, visual flight rules all the way and four SOB, (Souls On Board) Ed, myself and my sons, Terry and Kevin.

We were going down the Zorg en Hoop runway at 9:22. This one runway narrow field has about 1000 feet of hard surface and another 1000 feet of dirt/sod. The field elevation is about 10 feet above high tide. We used the entire hard surface and a few clods of sod then were up and on our way. After climbing out to 1200 feet, we began a turn to a south, southwest course and on to our first check point, Tafelberg. We leveled off at 1700 feet, just below the cloud layer. The bauxite mines at SURALCO and BILLITON passed under us while ahead and to the right we could see Zanderij International Airport. These mines and the airport were the object of some darts from Ernest Gann in his book, "Fate is the Hunter". Obviously Mr. Gann was not aware of the importance of these mines in the production of aluminum during WW II. It was more than possible that the airplane he was flying came out of a mine here in Suriname. The fact that SURALCO was now my bread and butter and a plane my transportation might have influenced my view of these holes in the ground.

As we flew on, hard roads turned into gravel, then to dirt, and then into trails, that disappeared into the jungle. Now it was only jungle occasionally broken by rivers, rapids or less frequent villages on the river. Hills began to rise (Suriname is flat level bush country to about 80 miles inland from the Atlantic) as well as the cloud cover so for the most part, a climbing attitude was maintained. The jungle is so complete and dense that any break can be seen at some distance. Tafelburg could be seen very easily in the distance and as it came under our right wheel, we turned to our next heading and check point at Kayserburg.

The jungle once again became a green mat broken only by hills, rivers and an occasional granite outcropping. This leg of the trip was over the most rugged country of the trip. Passing over the Kayserburg air strip, our check point, we turned to a heading that would take us to Sipaliwini. The land began to turn into rolling hills: the most rugged part was now behind us.

Kelly pointed out the village of Alalapadu off to our left and some distance ahead. I changed course to fly over the place that would be my major checkpoint on my walk. Shortly after leaving Alalapadu, the rolling hills turned into savanna and extended south. Then the Sipaliwini airport came into sight.

Our top altitude during the trip had been 2700 feet. We now started our descent and final approach. Ed took over the controls on base leg and proceeded to grease the bird in on the dirt strip. We taxied up to the tower and parked at 11:40, two hours and 18 minutes after takeoff.

The strip at Sipaliwini is part of a project called "Operation Grasshopper". It, like the fields we had flown over at Tafelburg and Kayserberg, are intended to help open up the interior. They are large enough to accommodate a DC 3 type aircraft and are manned and equipped with HF (High Frequency) radio. Sipaliwini is the southernmost of all, about 20 kilometers north of the border with Brazil.

There are no villages within reasonable walking distance of this place so the population is made up of the people who man the operation and an occasional guest. The buildings consist of the tower mounted on top of the radio and flight room, a small building for the generating plant, several buildings to house the personnel and supplies, and a guest house. The guest house is located some distance from the other buildings and has lights, water and sanitary facilities. The guest house is provided by the SLM and can be rented by reservation. Persons wishing to take short trips for hunting or fishing in the surrounding areas could live quite comfortably in the house.

After parking the plane, we all got out to stretch after the ride. I went to the tower and introduced myself and asked if the three men had arrived. The fellow in charge was not expecting us so when he heard the plane he cranked up the generator so he could use the radio. By the time he was set to use the radio, we were on the ground. In addition to not expecting us, he had not expected nor did he see my guides. We were the first people to come here in some time. Back at the plane, the moetete was unloaded and carried to the combination tower, radio, flight room. At about the same time, I noticed some movement on the far side of the field. The three guides had been sitting there shading themselves with a type of broad leaf like a banana leaf. It was obvious they had been there for some time but had not been noticed by the people living here. These men were sent here from Alalapadu on Thursday so I was satisfied they could find their way back.

Mr. Kelly, the boys and I had taken a lunch along. Terry and Kevin got air sick on the way here so had no desire to eat. (Apparently it was my flying of the plane, or lack of flying, that did not agree with them. On the return trip, they felt fine all the way.) I did not eat either so I took all three lunches to eat later that day. After eating, Mr. Kelly filled out a flight plan for the return. The three of them were on their way at 12:30.

182 returning to Paramaribo with Kelly, Terry, and Kevin

The guides and I took our gear to the guest house where things could be repacked. My supplies were dry foods so a maximum of meals could be made from a minimum of bulk weight. There was enough for all of us and if need be, we could buy food at the first village. It depended on what these men carried to provide game enroute. At 1:30, everything was repacked. These men were carrying their machetes in their hand so I hand-carried mine rather than pack it. I filled the canteen with water and we were on our way.

II

Sipaliwini to Pousoe Tirio, Brazil

Traveling in the savanna

Generally, this is where the jungle gives way to the savanna. The jungle becomes broken by small "islands" of savanna and it is on one of these "islands" where the airport is located. The main savanna is south and east of here. After leaving the rather small savanna that contains the airport, we entered a wooded area. Because of motor vehicles stationed at the airport, there were a few dirt roads venturing into the outer areas. The roads did not go very far before becoming well defined trails. We followed these trails for some distance. By three o'clock we had crossed the strip of jungle and entered into the main savanna.

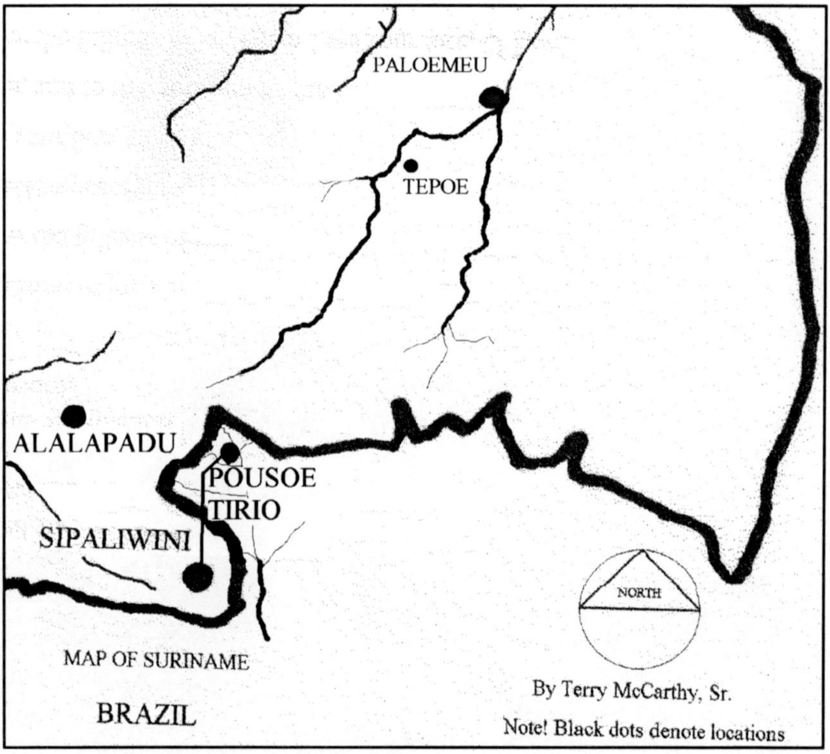

Route to Pousoe Tirio

This part of the savanna was rolling country with a few trees set at random on the hillsides: quite unconsciously, I expected cattle to be seen grazing there. Having lived in the cattle raising district of Costa Rica, where cattle were hanging on every hillside, it was more surprising not to see cattle. In the low areas between the hills, water gathered into ponds: here heavy marsh-type vegetation grew well over our heads. This grass-like vegetation was very sharp and could cut or rip through ordinary clothing. Animal trails were used for walking through these areas; we used our machetes to cut overhanging growth. These areas were wet enough that turtles were living here: we met a fairly large one. The guides wore long sleeved shirts and pants to protect them from the sharp grass. On the hillsides a variety of shorter grass grew, but was equally sharp. For anyone planning to travel very long in the savanna, heavy canvas-type clothes should be worn.

When I contacted Mr. Leavitt at Alalapadu, I indicated my intention of going first to Pousoe Tirio, Brazil then to Alalapadu. Before leaving the airport, I had asked the man in charge to determine if these three men had been instructed to go that way and he said they had. Not knowing the language of the guides has its drawbacks. (The travel between Alalapadu and Pousoe Tirio was a regular route: the travel from Sipaliwini and Pousoe Tirio was not a regularly traveled route.)

Pousoe Tirio is north and east of the Sipaliwini airport. While we were heading in the proper direction, several things indicated that the boys were not too sure of the exact route. After an hour in the savanna, one of the boys took off his moetete and went up on a prominent hill to take a look. In the direction we were moving, I could not see any jungle we could make before dark. It was difficult to imagine making camp out here in the savanna, fortunately we did not. He came back and said we should be more to the north: we then back-tracked into the jungle. Some 200 yards into the bush by a very small stream is where we set up camp. It was about 4:30.

Setting up camp consisted in clearing the ground of dead leaves and small plants in the area. Each guide seemed to have his own task and went about it in an industrious manner. We each needed a shelter. The jungle hammock I borrowed from Rambharos was set up to provide the 4th shelter. This jungle hammock had a roof and mosquito net. All I needed were two trees, the correct distance apart, to tie up the hammock and I was home.

The guides' shelters consisted of locating two trees the appropriate distance apart, about eight feet, the size seemed to be about three inches in diameter or larger, these two trees form the main support of the shelter. A branch, or small tree, was cut that was more than the distance between the two trees: this served as the roof ridge pole and was tied with vines about head high or higher. If two trees of the proper size and distance could not be found, they cut a tree of the proper size. The larger end was sharpened and driven into the ground at the proper distance from the tree, thus serving as the second tree.

Poles were driven into the ground about two feet on either side of the trees, forming the four corners, supporting the shelter.

There were now three uprights at each end: one tree and two poles.

Two other poles were cut and tied between the corner poles parallel to the ridge pole, but lower.

Two more poles were cut, about three feet long, and tied between the three uprights on either end.

The three roof poles and end poles formed the frame of the roof.

Camp with the shelters completed

The next task was to get branches of about ¾ inch in diameter or less and about four feet long. These were bowed over the ridge pole and tied to the two side poles. These branches were spaced at random distances along the length of the roof poles and extended to the outside, forming eaves. Palm fronds are now placed on these supports starting on the outside and stacked to the ridge pole. The last frond is placed on top, providing a roof that sheds water. The hammock is now suspended between the main uprights, the moetete is set under one end of the shelter and the guide is now home.

The jungle has a very dense canopy that allows the sunlight in only when the sun is high. By the same way, no matter how bad the storm or how hard it rains, the rain in the jungle always comes straight down. By building the shelter some three to four feet wide, the men could stay in their hammock and be dry. The time required to build the three shelters was about 20 minutes, now a fire was built and tea was started. It seemed these people had done this before.

My evening meal consisted of my lunch sandwich and the two my sons left for me. The men like their tea with plenty of saccharin. Because of our newness to each other, we were watching and feeling out each other. They had their supply of food and I had mine, it was just a matter of our getting used to each other. Neither knew if the other would eat the other's food.

We all took a bath in the nearby stream and were ready to turn in. After getting into the hammock, the men started to sing some of their songs. It was dark and the jungle sounds were in full swing: the small campfire and the songs made a very satisfying end to the first day. The younger guide began reciting something which went on for some time. About 9:00 they got up, stoked up the fire, ate some more, then turned in for the night.

August 3

After a fair night's sleep, life came back to the camp about 5:30. The guides started the day by singing. The fire was rekindled, and the first order of business was to make coffee. After a short breakfast, we moved out of our first camp at 7:15.

Backtracking continued until 8:20 at which time we arrived back at the trail we had passed yesterday, we did lose some time but are now on the proper trail. This trail is fairly well-defined and at 9:30 it led us to an old camp. This camp had been set up for a number of people. A considerable amount of military type gear was lying about. A number of square five gallon tins, also a length of 3/8" wire rope, (cable) was found with an eye spliced in one end. Apparently the group that stayed here had some heavy equipment that required a wire rope of this size. The guides were looking for various goodies to take which the people had left behind—exchanging some boots, pants and shirts. Tea was made on a little kerosene stove. Leaving this camp at 10:15, the trail was pursued till 11:20 at which time a 10 minute water and cassava bread break was taken.

Our trail took us out of the jungle back into the savanna. Two things about the Indians have been confirmed: one, they prefer to stay in the jungle where it is cool and two they are never far from water. This had been told me by a number of people: it was now confirmed.

While in the savanna this time, I took a compass shot of a prominent hill some distance to the north. It was a very prominent point in the direction we were heading: I felt it would be a good reference every time we came to a clearing. While well-intentioned, it didn't work out that way. We were in this piece of savanna for about an hour then back into the jungle where we stayed for the next few days.

Before going back into the jungle, we heard an airplane take off from Sipaliwini. When we were able to see the plane, it was fairly high and heading north. The plane was a De Havilland Twin Otter (a twin engine short field aircraft used quite extensively in the bush) from the SLM (Suriname Air Lines) on a regular flight to supply these outlying Grasshopper fields.

Back into the jungle, we pursued the same trail. Very shortly we heard birds up ahead. One of the guides was carrying a 16-gauge single shot shotgun. The boys went hunting and shortly there were two shots—they returned with two birds. The boys told me they were okos which in the Trio language is turkey. Most surprising of this whole episode was that after the shooting, the shotgun was cleaned.

The oko is about the size of an average chicken. For the most part, it is all black except the bill which is a bright orange to a yellow in color. While these birds can be very quiet, they make enough noise when flying that they manage to give themselves away.

Progress was good and when we stopped again I took the opportunity to stretch out and relax: take a snooze. My feet were starting to hurt so my boots came off. You can imagine how overjoyed I was to see a couple of nice blisters well started. Needless to say, the guides saw them also. The boots went back on and we continued.

At 2:30 our trail became a rather large fallen tree that crossed a nice river and ended at an abandoned camp on the far side. This camp had been set up for a large group to live in for an extended period of time. The camp was most likely for a Geological group or possibly a group to gather balata (a rubber-like substance). Rather than going through the building of a shelter as last night, we each selected a suitable shelter and moved in. Making this camp was a rather short project.

One of the men took some shells and the shotgun and left to do some trail scouting and hunting. The other two started to clean the turkeys, build a fire while I made coffee, took a swim in the river and washed some clothes. About 5:00 the turkey was declared finished. The Indians had a small cooking pot with a wire handle and a cover. This is not packed but is carried by hand. The two turkeys were cut up and placed in the pot, water added, then some dry peppers and lastly rice. This is simmered over the open fire. When finished, the meat is still somewhat tough, not much more than some fryer chickens I have had. Cassava bread was broken up and put in with the juice and made a good meal with one exception: the dry peppers they put in were enough to burn the guts of a

Mexican. With the help of half of the river, it was a good meal. The boys thought it was funny but they did back off on the peppers for the rest of the trip. While some hot is enjoyable, there is a limit to the damn stuff.

The hunter/scout returned with a monkey at about 5:30 and declared he had found the proper trail. While he was eating, the others started to clean the monkey. This particular type of monkey, while about the normal-size monkey, had very black hair. The most distinctive part about this fellow was the hair on his head: it was parted in the middle. It looked like someone had taken a comb, parted his hair and combed it nicely to both sides. The animal is cleaned much like a pig or chicken. It is put in hot water and then the hair is removed, not skinned. Some of the meat is cooked and eaten and the remainder is smoked for future use.

Guide holding a black monkey; in the background are turkeys by the fire

Because camp was so easily set up and we were a little early too, there was some time to look about and get a better feel of this new environment. This camp had several types of shelters: some for storage, others for living and those that could be for a mess hall, cooking and supplies. Most of them had log floors with dirt packed between them and some dirt on top. The thatch roofing extended over the log floor thus assuring adequate drainage even in some real wet weather. A considerable amount of gear had been left here, most notably the number of kerosene lanterns and an amount of kerosene that could be used in them. That night we had lanterns to light the paths of our "village". About 8:00 it was time for a cup of tea and a turkey wing. Before turning in, an inspection was held on my feet. They almost looked worse than the turkey or the monkey. I put some sulfa ointment on them, some dry socks, then into the hammock. Again there was some singing and recitation then just the sounds of the night.

The sounds of the night were many and varied from an almost chirp down to a basso profundo and lower. I wish I could see the owner of that basso. One night while lying in the hammock, the frogs and toads took over the bandstand for the only real performance during the trip. After the preliminary tune-up a pair of these fellows got the beat and damn if they didn't get Tchaikovsky's Nut Cracker Suite kicked off. They were going after the Dance of the Sugar Plumb Fairies with the bassoons going back and forth.

They kept this up for some time in perfect time but the flute player didn't get the message. After a brilliant start but getting no help, one of them just burped and said to hell with it. There were varying attempts the rest of the night to start up but they never could get organized again.

August 4.

Awake at 6:00, the day was again started with songs and prayers. Breakfast consisted of coffee, tea, turkey, rice and cassava bread. We were on our way by 8:15.

An hour later, the men stopped and two of them went on ahead without their moetetes. We had been in a relatively flat country for some time. The bush was not too difficult to travel in or to cut where needed. Very obviously, we were on a trail of some kind. There is an established trail between Pousoe Tirio and Alalapadu, we were not on it and very obviously the boys didn't know where it was.

I was carrying the most detailed maps available of the area. These had been made from aerial photos some ten to fifteen years ago. Aside from the larger rivers in the area and very prominent elevations, it had very little relation to the jungle floor. The aerial photos only show the canopy of the jungle and not what is on the ground. At least an attempt was going to be made to plot the walk. Last night in camp and at odd moments like this, it was a good pastime to try and locate where we were or had been. During these ventures, a few spots were found that had a degree of reliability. The compass was always near at hand, the string tied around my neck with the compass in my shirt pocket for quick and easy use. I checked the first map and made a guess as to where we were. I concluded that we had run off this map so I pulled out the next one. An estimated scientific guess located our present location.

A WAG is called a "Wild Ass Guess". If we wish to be more specific, we make a SWAG, which is a "Scientific Wild Ass Guess". So we will SWAG our way to our destination. Yesterday, when we left the jungle and went on the savanna, I was able to pick out a very distinctive hill or mountain. This was about three to five degrees east of north. At this time, we had not emerged out of the jungle enough to see that point again.

After an hour the guides returned and we were off again, going generally in the westerly direction. Then the boys swung to the south. When that happened, I stopped them and swung them back to the north. This happened a number of times before we kept on a northern heading. There was no question of being lost but now we were all in the same boat. The compass was what we were going to use till something else came along. In trying to figure out what the problem was, aside from being lost, only three things came to mind; one, the trail we should be on is to the east; two, the trail they had used between Alalapadu and Sipaliwini is to the west and; three;

the boys decided to go directly to Alalapadu, possibly because of my feet. To better understand the situation, some knowledge of the lay of the land is necessary.

The border between Suriname and Brazil is the continental divide. All the water on the Surname side flows to the north and west to the Atlantic. All the water on the Brazil side flows south and east to the Amazon River. So far in our trip, all the water has been flowing to the west on the Suriname side. By going north, the hills were met head on. (The part we were in, the border ran north by northwest thus accounting for the boys wanting to go west or south to get away from the hills). By moving west and south, it would take us out of the sharp hills into more gently rolling hills.

By going my way, north and east, a series of low but rugged hills were encountered. It would seem that we were on or near the border. At one time I was sure that we had crossed over when we came to a stream that was flowing north and east. Further on it made a swing back to the west. I was chugging and puffing like an old steam engine and had the boys stop so I could rest at the top of each and every hill. The canteen ran out of water and damn, did I get dry. After some time, we came to a beautiful mountain pool, even a can of iced-down beer could not have looked better. The time was about 2:00. An hour later and some distance further, camp was set up. Again a stream is at hand at the proper time so camp was made following the same procedures as the first night.

After camp was set up, I went to the little stream and took a bath. It had a sandy bottom so I sat in the nice white sand and watched the soap bubbles merrily go on their way polluting the pure natural countryside. Once camp is made, my boots come off and I go barefoot and watch very carefully just where the foot is placed. I am not overly interested in walking through a pack of ants or stepping on a scorpion. After the bath, the two messy companions get first aid. Even after such tender loving care, they bothered me all night so didn't sleep too well.

August 5.
Kevin's Birthday

It rained easy all night so everything was dripping in the morning. Even after several days of no rain, it is still damp in the jungle and always cool. The only way to get clothes dry is to hang them by the fire. This morning there were no dry socks, so damp ones were put on then with some force the boots went on. It may be necessary to customize these boots. Before sitting on a log to eat and write some notes, it was necessary to move a smoked and dried monkey head. The monkey head, hands and feet are not packed but are carried along to munch on while traveling.

Moving out of camp at the usual 8:00, we came to a river in about an hour. This is apparently the Akalapi River from its size and direction. We started downstream in what I expected was a search for a crossing. After some time we came to three shelters that had been built and used some time ago. A short time later we stopped so I could take some pictures of the river.

Picture taking is quite an operation because the camera is kept in a plastic bag. Because of the constant high humidity in the jungle, every effort must be made to keep the film and camera dry. In order to do this, a dehydrated powder called "KALK" was recommended. Toilet tissue was used to make packets of kalk. The tissue contained the kalk but was still porous enough to absorb the moisture. The film was kept in the tins and boxes then placed in a plastic bag with the packets of this kalk. Exposed film was placed back in the tins and returned to this bag with the other exposed film. In this way, it was not necessary to open the bag too often. The bag was large enough so it could be folded into a water-proof pack. The camera was in a separate bag that also had a number of packets of kalk. When not in use, the camera case and the strap were rolled up, put in a bag, the excess air forced out and the bag folded over. All of this was stuffed into a canvas bag, holding the things normally expected to be used during the day. Usually pictures were taken in conjunction with regular stops or in camp. When something special came our way, we stopped to take pictures. If the camera is taken out and shots taken immediately, there is no problem, if however, there is a lapse of time, the lens fogged up and it was necessary to wait for the lens to clear.

Stopping this time was just such a case. By the time the camera was out and I was in a position to take the picture, the lens had fogged. Whenever the camera came out, the boys would move off to the side. They were not afraid of the camera but seemed to think that I did not want them in the picture. The actual time involved in taking a few shots could easily run from 10 to 15 minutes.

While putting the camera away, the boys came back where I was standing. When all was ready to move on, they said we were going back and move upstream, so again we backtracked. We passed the three shelters and on to where we had first come to the river. Going upstream, we maintained a fairly constant easterly heading. After traveling for a while, the feet and boots got together and began to work in union. The trail by the river was a very good one and while slow because of my feet, progress was good.

One of the men went on ahead. After a while some chopping could be heard up ahead. When we came to the place, our friend Yanamane was way up the tree happily cutting away in the honey tree. He asked for the pot so he could put honey in it. The contents were removed and the pot was sent up to him. Piri went up to help.

Climbing trees is quite an art. About 10 to 12 feet of vine is cut. The vine is made into a two to two and a half foot loop. This is doubled over so it uses all 10 - 12 feet of the vine. Then the feet are placed in the loop. It seemed that the actual size of the loop is determined by the size of the tree. Placing a foot on either side of the tree, the vine gives an added amount of traction. In climbing the tree, the user pulls up with his hands then pulls his feet up with the vine. Then up with his hands again. This is similar to shinnying up a tree but much faster. It is much like a pole climber but instead of the climbing spuds, the vine serves the purpose. These boys are able to go up a tree like a ladder when using the vine around their feet. In descending, the tree, the vine is used like a braking devise. For the most part, it is used just to control the speed of the descent. If the vine broke, it could cause some excitement.

I would estimate that about a quart of honey was taken from that tree. We all sat down and using cassava bread "spooned" the honey from the pot. This is nothing but the greatest and improves the taste of the cassava. Fortunately, these bees are very docile. The bee is only ¾ th to one inch long and not aggressive. While eating this most welcomed treat, the bees landed on us and got honey—sure glad the entire swarm didn't come down.

While sitting near the river, eating honey, some birds started to make noise. They seemed to be heading in our general direction. For a joke, Pori started to call them, they seemed to dig what he was saying and shortly about four of them came into view. We kept eating honey while the birds kept on coming; when one of them came in close enough, Pori lifted up the shotgun and added one more bird to the pack. When asked the name of the bird, none seemed to have one. The bird looked very much like a grouse by color, design and size. After I had my quota of honey and cassava, I took my right boot off because the little toe was giving me more of a bad time than it should. As it turned out the blister, which was rather large, had broken the day before. Last evening while enjoying soaking in that nice stream, sand had entered that hole and filled the former blister with nice white sand. Now, with the aid of the hunting knife, the sand was removed. For some reason, the sand did not help the healing process very much. Twenty minutes were spent here enjoying all of this.

Continuing on, we came upon some Brazil nuts. About the only way I can explain them is to compare them to a grapefruit. The Brazil nut shell is about the same size as a grapefruit. When opened up, the individual nuts fit together like the slices in a grapefruit and are about the same size and shape. The similarity is only in overall design and no more. The outer shell is hard like hell—the individual "slices" are hard but the outer shell is much harder.

It may be a good time to explain the difference between the

machete I was carrying and the cutlass the guides had. The cutlass is much heavier than my machete. The blade is about 18 to 20 inches long and the end is curved up to a point. Having a heavy end gives this knife a lot of carry-through on the cut. It is much better for cutting wood than the machete. In the process of breaking the outer shell of the Brazil nut, the guides held the shell on a log, hauled back with the cutlass and hit the outer shell of the thing. The blade would sing like mad while they were cutting or busting the outer shell. I just stood back and watched.

The boys then gave me a quick lesson on how to open these nuts without a nut cracker. Using the machete, I cut two of the three edges and took out the meat. These were the first nuts we had encountered but after that we came across more.

The honey and nuts were most enjoyable but their presence re-established that we were off the track. Honey is very much in demand and any area traveled by the Indians is picked clean. While they may not clean up the nuts, one would expect to see signs of the shells having been broken open.

We followed the river upstream for the remainder of the day. Our heading was swinging more to the north. At 3:30 we crossed the river and began to set up camp. This camp site was near a clearing which had been made when some trees fell down. For the most part, the jungle is like woods found in most temperate zones. It is generally open with small brush and undergrowth. Trees grow straight and tall with few lower branches. These tree tops form a canopy that is more like a mat or carpet. Very little sunlight gets through and then only during midday. Occasionally, a large tree will fall, either being too rotten to stand or possibly hit by lightning. When large trees come down, because the tops are so interwoven, they bring down a number of other trees with them. Depending on the size and location, these trees can clean a rather large area. The clearing we were camping by was such a place. We had good sunlight until about 5:30. This good fortune allowed me to get some clothes dry.

After setting up camp, the boys made a fire and we had some tea and coffee then the three of them decided to go off to look about and fish. For myself, I took a bath, washed some clothes and sat in the sunlight. I also decided to have a fire of my own. For some reason, our shelters were further apart than usual so if a fire were closer it would be easier to have coffee and dry some clothes after sundown.

Having built a number of fires in the woods, I considered myself at least adequate in this skill. Fires out here are very important and they are an art in themselves, so no time like the present to go into the subject of fires. The Indians carry a piece of resin from some particular tree. At first I thought they were stones or pieces of rock. In building the fire, dry wood is placed in a small pile, a match is used to start the resin on fire, the resin is placed under the dry wood and presto, a fire. One of the first things I noticed when I first met the Indians was an acrid smoke smell. After sitting by one of their fires, the sinuses are thoroughly cleaned and all dirt and dust from the past four years is flushed from your eyes: there is no more questions as to why they have this smell. After the dry wood is started, a select type of wood is used. The wood most commonly used is a small branch or sapling, about one to two inches in diameter. They use only the green or nearly green wood. To get this wood to really burn, a set of leather lungs is required. Once this wood is burning, it makes a fire hot like hell. The only wood like it for heat would be a mesquite fire. The fire is kept small and the pot is suspended from a stick of wood. As the wood burns, the pieces of wood are moved in, and this is the art. It is possible to have a small white hot fire and if the pieces are not moved in, the fire goes out, leaving a hole burned in the middle.

My attempt at a fire was to gather the wood that looked like it may burn. Some large sticks or pieces were split and set where the fire was to be built. I went over to the fire the guides had and borrowed some of their burning wood and carried them over to my place. This was followed by some tender loving care and a lot of blowing. When a nice flame was going, my attention was turned over to other things. When attention was again turned to the fire, there was a pink eye under some black sticks looking at a tiny whisper of smoke above—back to the TLC and blowing. This was repeated a number of times and I did manage to make a pot of coffee. Some clothes were hung near the smoke so if they were not dry they would at least be bug-proofed.

I was taking vitamin pills as an added helper but as usual they gave me some problems. Normally any radical change in dieting routine will give me a bit of constipation or the runs. This time it was constipation. Not liking to take medicine for every ache or pain, the vitamins were now taken only occasionally. Later a pill was taken for the constipation.

Just before dark, the men came back bringing a few fish with them. Not feeling too all-fired good, I just got into the hammock. This was the end of our third full day on the trail and we had not met anyone.

August 6.

After a good night sleep, breakfast and an extra cup of coffee, we were ready to go. My oldest son, Terry, gave me a canvas water bag, the type commonly used in the western states. It was taken along because it could be handy and when empty takes up very little room. Each evening, after taking a bath, I filled it and hung it near my hammock. This saved extra trips to get water. The bag also keeps the water cool. In the morning I used it to clean up, wash up and brush my teeth. When repacking, the contents were emptied, and the bag packed. This morning the contents were very ceremoniously dumped on my fire (well almost a fire) so the damn thing would not start the jungle on fire.

Continuing up the same river, now a creek, in an east/northeast direction, the land again turned into hills. When traveling in this type of rolling hills, things take on a sameness—we continued on.

At about 11:30, much to our surprise, we met a family on the trail. Even the jungle is getting crowded. When they first saw us, they started jabbering, running around and carrying on for some time. They had some dogs which added to the ball. The group consisted of a man and his wife, their two sons, the older of the two boys' wife and two very small children: seven people and about 10 dogs. After talking to my guides, the older gentleman came over to me and started to talk. I said something in Spanish and he answered in Portuguese so then I knew they were from Brazil. Between his Portuguese and my Spanish, we could understand each other—a little. He said we should make Pousoe Tirio by noon tomorrow.

To say the least, this raised hell with my time schedule because my plans were to be in Alalapadu tomorrow. From my calculations, a minimum of one and a half days had been lost by our wanderings. Well at this point, there was not much chance in getting there so may as well spend a day in Brazil when we're this close. The only problem was that the timetable I had given my wife would by now be two days off. There would be no communications with her until Alalapadu.

At this time, Pousoe Tirio was not much more than a name on the map. My information was that it was a full mission with a landing strip like Sipaliwini.

Traveling in the same general E-N-E direction, we came to some bush that had ground water standing as far as we could see ahead. Some time ago it was discovered that dry boots, socks and feet were better than wet ones. With all the water ahead, there was no way to keep dry. The boots and socks came off and the pants were rolled up. If the canteen was emptied out, it would help my balance, so it was emptied. I started to pick my way through the brush. Each of the men took a cup of water and carried it. This water and bush was about a kilometer wide. While walking, staggering through this, one of the Indians, Piri, started to whistle "On Top of Old Smoky". Then, like someone turned on a switch, we stepped into the sunlight and the savanna.

The sun was hot and it was possible to see for miles. After the cool dark jungle, this was a real change. The water the men were carrying was put in the canteen when we came out of the bush. These guides were taking very good care of me. At the edge of the savanna there was a path—this smooth hard surface felt so good that I kept on walking barefoot. We had not been on the path too long when we saw tire tracks. Some people had said that there was a special jeep used here for traveling in the savanna. A short distance further, traffic had been heavy enough to start forming two ruts–a regular highway.

This part of the savanna was relatively level with small patches of wooded areas here and there. The road continued on through and around the wooded areas. As mentioned before, savanna grass is sharp. The grass that hung over the path cut my feet and, worst of all, hit the open sores on my feet. I had thoroughly enjoyed about one and a half kilometers of barefoot walking but then decided to put the boots on again. After washing and drying the feet, some salve was applied then dry socks. The boots went on hard and walking was just plain hell. My pace slowed to about half and each step was a real bitch.

At about this time, an armadillo crossed our path. I hollered to the boys and one of them ran out and killed it with a cutlass: one more bit of game for the pot.

After an hour of plodding, it was quite obvious that the boots would not work out. The boots came off but the socks stayed on. This felt much better and the grass did not get to the feet through the socks. After walking on the savanna for a short time, the sun felt good and hot, it was most welcome: I decided to put on my hat. There was no need for sunglasses because the sun was behind us. About an hour before sunset, small black flies started to show up. This is another reminder of some of my informants, also a confirmation of why Indians don't like to travel in the savanna. I had been told to be off the savanna an hour and a half before sundown. Strangely, insects in the jungle were almost nonexistent. Here in the savanna, the damn flies like to pick one up and eat them at one setting. I put on my long sleeved shirt and turned the sleeves down. In order to protect the back of my neck, I took out a large red "farmers" handkerchief, put a corner under my hat and left the rest of it flop. The sides were later tucked around the straps that went over my head and to the back pack, moetete. This effectively kept them off my head and face. I may have looked like Lawrence of Arabia, sin camel, but it kept the flies off.

The distance from where we left the jungle to the village is an estimated 8 kilometers. Our arrival was at 6:45 in the evening, about 18 hours ahead of the estimate of the old man on the trail but two days late because of the detour. At dark, we heard a diesel generator start up. This was the first real evidence of the location of the village—this chug-a-lug diesel was a most welcome sound.

About a kilometer before we entered the village, the boys took a pack of supplies and laid them by some bushes on the side of the road. (The trail had turned into a full-blown road.) We then proceeded on to the village but stopped on the edge. The boys let go five shots from the shotgun to announce our arrival.

III

Missao Pousoe Tirio, Brazil

The village, with its inevitable square, was situated on a small knoll. The square was somewhat illuminated by a few yellow lights which revealed a number of people and a lot of dogs. My three guides melted into the people and huts leaving me alone to find whoever I was going to find. Aside from the fact that no one was expecting me, I no doubt was a sight to behold. My pack and my boots were on my back, clothes were dirty, a day's whiskers, (I shaved every other day) socks on my feet, a slow stiff walk and pooped out.

On the far side of the square, was a building more conspicuous than the others. Built of cement blocks, better lighted, it had a concentration of activities. Crossing over the square, it became apparent that this building was the center of the village. A group of non-Indians were preparing to eat so my timing was flawless. No one could speak English so we took off on the Spanish/Portuguese route. The man in charge turned out to be a Catholic priest. I explained to him that I was alone with the three Trios from Alalapadu. Father asked if I wished to wash up or eat first—washing up sounded best.

Going off to clean up, Fr. explained that the facilities were not very modern but I assured him that modern facilities were not necessary. We went into what seemed to be his quarters. The front room had a hammock, crucifix, a statue of the Blessed Virgin Mary, several religious articles, a set of powerful two-way radios, books, papers, magazines, a scoped rifle (seven or eight mm) and a shot gun. Passing into the next room that contained various types of supplies and a yellow light, Fr. pointed to a door leading to a shed. He reached in and turned on a light and revealed the most beautiful shower in existence.

While getting ready to shower, we went over generalities. There were two other priests with him but they were presently at other missions. This priest was Frei Cirilo Maas, OFM a Franciscan priest from Germany. This delighted me and I in turn told him I was a Franciscan, a member of the Third Order of St. Francis. As a member of the Third Order, I wore a cord around my waist which I showed him. With a big roar of laughter, he went around the corner into his living quarters and presently stepped back in with a jug in one hand and two glasses in the other. Following the advice of St. Francis, I accepted what was offered. There was also a brother and a visiting priest here. This was Missao Pousoe Tirio, C. P. BELEM/Para/Brazil.

After showering, Fr. provided me with some ill-fitting but dry clothes and a pair of sandals. We returned to the main building and sat down to enjoy a very good meal. It consisted of local (Brazil) cooking flavored with some of the good friar's German cooking: this included some sour milk dishes.

Between the time of showering and eating, my supplies that were being carried by the guides, were rather unceremoniously dumped on the floor of Father's storage room. These were picked up and carried to the guest house where I was going to stay. The guest house was a regular thatched hut by the village square with a small porch and two rooms. I stepped on to the porch, opened the door and chose the room on the right: one yellow light and a dry place to sleep. My supplies were dumped here for the time being because there were more important things to be taken care of at this moment.

As mentioned before, constipation was becoming a problem. When I found out that we would be in Tirio in the near future, some pills that would help the matter were taken. Hearing some rumbles earlier in the evening, it seemed rather reasonable to determine the location of the required sanitary facilities. Once the location was known, it was time to get back to the guest house and set up for the night.

It took some time to rig up the hammock. These people are short and the buildings are built accordingly: their hammocks are built to those requirements. The only way my hammock would fit was to hang it from corner to corner in the room. Having set up my house for the night, it was time to take a journey to the building at the end of the path. (A tourist brochure would describe this as "a native hut with two rooms and a path.").

The outhouse was built over a narrow but deep gully so when it rained real hard the toilet would flush. With the hope of arriving at a solution to my difficult problem, having used the squatters rights in the jungle, I had really been looking forward to sitting down and enjoying the relief. Moving (no joke) down the path, the flashlight beam gave the building the once over. I was admiring the looks of this well-built wooden structure. The building also had a light inside but, except for the top vent (not a star or a quarter moon), there was very little light showing: a very sound building. After knocking to be sure there were no inhabitants, I opened the door.

To my complete and unending surprise, there was no throne but rather a landing pad in the center of the floor. This landing pad was a square porcelain casting mounted flush with the floor. The inner portion sloped down to a round hole in the back, the front slope was more gradual, the back more abrupt. On the front portion were cast two foot pads, lower than the floor, but well above the target area. These foot pads were of the proper shape, small at the heel, broader for the front part of the foot with the toes pointing outward. The pads are raised high enough so it would be uncomfortable underfoot if stood on improperly. This was a built-in design feature to ensure a holding pattern in only the proper direction. This foreign import had one thing going for it: it sure gave a hell of a target area.

After reconnoitering the area, I laid a plan of attack. First of all, it would be necessary to disrobe. The thought of going in there with hobbles on only invited disaster. The most comforting part of this comfort house was the fact that the foot pads were tractionized. Going in barefoot also allowed for a better foothold. If anyone slipped and fell in that porcelain monster complete with hobbles, I am sure it would require dismantling the whole damn building to get them out. To add to the fun, there were no hand holds of any kind. After a very moving performance, I headed back down the path.

On the return trip, I passed the combination center where Father and some other people were gathered. He and I visited for a while, met some of the people and had a chance to look the place over again. While Father did not smoke too much, there seemed to be an Indian man or woman asking him for a cigarette all the time. At the going rate, he must have gone through a carton per day. Anyhow, Father always gave out as requested and if nothing else, did assure himself a fresh smoke at all times.

For various reasons, sleep accounted for only about three hours of the night. Every damn dog in the village had a fight that either started ended or took place just outside my very thin-walled house. Two additional trips to the porcelain monster took their time.

August 7.

When my watch said it was time to roll out of the hammock, I did and proceeded to get cleaned up. Last night Father told me the hour for Mass. I wanted to go so made sure I was ready on time. Stepping out of the house, it seemed odd that there was no activity at all. Then I realized that these people were not on Suriname time.

This did allow time to walk around the village without anyone to bother me. The exact geographical location of this village depends on the map one is looking at. It is, however, on the Perue (or Paru) River and in the savanna northeast of Sipaliwini. The river travels south and empties into the Amazon River.

The town is built on a small knoll with the village square more or less occupying the top. On all sides of the square were various huts or buildings of all sizes shapes and designs. This village has been here for sometime as can be seen by the number of buildings and general progress in and around the area. Chickens were well established and we even had some eggs last night. There were some cattle but mostly buffalo that furnished milk and also provided some butter.

To the rear of the village was a saw mill driven by a diesel engine. Nearby was the diesel power plant, the one we heard as we approached the village last night, which provided all of the lights. The power plant was operated on the as-needed basis. It was shut down last night about 11:00. Nearby was a machine shop and equipment repair shop that had a surprising amount of equipment: machines such as a metal lathe, drill press, grinder and hydraulic press were basically "manufactured" in contrast to a very representative amount of "home-made" equipment. A clay oven equipped with a metal door was built for heating irons and such things.

Continuing on this early morning walk, I came upon the maker of the tire tracks we saw yesterday at the edge of the savanna. It was a Mercedes tractor, somewhat of a cross between a tractor and a pickup. It was driven by a diesel engine and mounted on large, widely-spaced tires. With this high-centered clearance, it was well suited for traveling or working on the savanna. Mounted on the front of the tractor was an "A" frame arrangement which could be raised or lowered hydraulically. This lift must have been used to lift logs. Nearby was a trailer which could be hitched to the tractor.

Circulating back to the river and following the much-used road to the river, I found a well-built bridge made from two inch and four inch lumber. The bridge was built to accommodate the Mercedes tractor and trailer: possibly 100 feet long and about five feet above the water. On the other side of the river, the road turned right onto the savanna; some distance further, it turned left to parallel a dirt/sod airstrip. The airstrip followed the natural contour of the savanna. In this case, it went up and over a small rise and disappeared into the savanna beyond: the road continued along the runway to the top of the rise. Several buildings were located at this point. The airport operator lived here with some buildings for storage and most prominent of all was the "control tower". The savanna continued on to the east, rising and falling off in the distance ending in some jungle-covered hills 10 to 15 miles away.

Upstream of the bridge, was a home-made barge constructed out of two 55 gallon drums. The barge was anchored to the shore but not in the flow of the stream. A plank gave access from the shore to the barge. On deck, an electrically driven pump was mounted which pushed water from the river to a tank set on a tower in the center of the village. This was the source of the shower water and several other outlets in the village.

At the proper time, I ventured into the church. The church was a round thatched-roof pole building built on the side of the square away from the river. A third of the church, the side facing the square, was covered with woven mats from the ground to where the roof joins the wall. The roof reminded me of a funnel because it was like a cone with an extra tassel on top. The altar was set up in the center of this walled portion. The remaining two thirds of the church wall was formed by benches of split wooden sticks with openings for the people to pass in and out. Split stick benches filled the body of the church to the altar.

Mission church at Pousoe Tirio Brazil

No doubt the church was used for more than having Mass. The building was not used at night so chickens, birds and dogs were the night residents. As I waited for Father to come and offer Mass, I read my Liturgical Prayer.

From the time of my arrival at the church, things were never dull. Someone came in and very unceremoniously removed all of the night residents. Various Indians came in, some young some old, and a good number of in-betweens. The three guides came with the other young men. Later some of the people I met last night came in: four nuns, all of them members of the local Brazilian order of Christ Crucified, followed by the Papal Volunteer (somewhat like the US Peace Corps), a young man with an inexhaustible supply of energy, then a pharmacist and a visiting priest.

I met the Papal Volunteer, from Austria I believe, last night as he breezed through the eating area. This morning he bounded into church, took a baby from its mother and began to play with him (they all have bare butts so no problem with identification of gender). When Mass started, the little fellow was all played out and went to sleep, in his mothers arms. During the Mass, the Volunteer was very attentive but was always quick to retrieve a run-away baby.

Father had shaved and was in good spirits when he came in to say Mass. At about 6:30, he began my first Mass in the Portuguese language. Almost all of the people, young and old, had small notebooks to use at Mass. These people said all of the responses in Portuguese and sang songs, some of which were in the Trio language. In addition to the Mass, which was special in itself, the new language and the songs made this a very special occasion for me. After Mass and Communion, it is my practice to stay and pray for a short time in church. Surprisingly, most of the Indians stayed and, with the use of their notebooks, classes were held.

After Mass, Father, the visiting priest, the pharmacist, the sisters and I ate breakfast. Afterwards we talked, had some more coffee and watched the village come to life. Fires that had been kept overnight were stoked and the village had breakfast. Now, off to work. The Papal Volunteer started up the Mercedes, hooked up the trailer, which was being filled to capacity with workers—men, women and children. These people were taken out to various locations for work at farming, lumber and cement work. Off they went up the road I had entered the village on last night.

Mercedes tractor with trailer being loaded with families to go to work in the fields.

After a bad night, getting more sleep now was a good idea, however, some other things had to be done. First, find a woman to wash some of my clothes, then have the pharmacist clean up my feet, medicate and patch them. After accomplishing these two things, I went back to the guest house. By now, the village was quiet and the house was still cool. I stepped in, locked the door and set about making a bed. The room that I used to hang the hammock in had a counter on two sides about two feet wide and waist high. The top was made of split saplings like the benches in the church. The hammock was taken down and put on the counter, then using some clothes that did not require washing, some low spots were filled in and I had a tolerable bed. After testing the thing for stability, I laid down, stretched out as best as I could, burped and woke up two hours later. I felt a hell of a lot better and was ready to move. During my nap, it had rained and the scattered clouds produced showers part of the morning. The washed clothes were on the porch so I laid them out where the sun could hit them but not very likely the rain. Then off again to see what was going on in the village.

At various places there was some activity but not much. The head sister had some women and children helping her sweep the village square. This is a very common practice, all leaves, sticks, twigs and of course the dog droppings are swept off the bare hard surface of the town square. This, however, was to be a very thorough job and nothing was to be missed.

Saw mill at the mission

At Mass this morning, there was a young Indian man who had a number of strings of beads on his arms and legs. His loin cloth was new and long but his hair was cut short like the men usually seen in the cities. I found him in various places in the machine repair shop. Now he was wearing coveralls and seemed rather at home with the mechanical part of the village. I had the opportunity to talk to him and also to others about him. He had been sent to a technical school in some large city, possibly in Belem. After learning the trade, he came back here. I was in the mechanical training field so I was very interested in him and wished we could spend a few days together.

He was very sharp, about 20 to 23 years old and very capable but also needed help in some areas. Seeing this fellow and the general condition of all the equipment at the mission, I was impressed by the way the local people were moving into the mechanical age.

Father was in his room sitting by the two-way radio. His was a truly Franciscan cell, room, quarters, hermitage or whatever: it had that joyous organized confusion. Father Cirilo Hass, OFM had been in Brazil for ten years and here in Pousoe Tirio on and off for five years. He, along with the visiting priest and me, became somewhat involved in a conversation about Suriname history, the bauxite industry and various other things. Father, at the time, was also in radio contact with Belem and a cargo/passenger plane enroute here. During the pauses for his radio contact, I had the opportunity to look over his cell. Many of the things that could not be seen last evening now were given the once-over. His selection of books contained mostly classics but there were also a good number on raising cattle, lumber and farm products; worn magazines and periodicals had equal status with the classics. His prayer books, Mass missal and spiritual books were obviously not lost in the pile but occupied the top of the piles and easily accessible. During the conversation and when not on the radio, Father was busy fixing the automatic rope rewind for an outboard motor.

From bits and pieces of conversation in the room and on the radio, it became apparent that the Father Visitor of the Franciscan Order was coming in on the plane. They said the Visitor could speak English. I knew some Franciscans stationed in Manaus. These Franciscans were connected to the Sacred Heart Province in Chicago. Additional conversation established the Fr. Visitor was known to me. The plane was due to arrive at noon, their time. This information provided the reason for the added effort in cleaning up the village square.

In the hopes of pinpointing the exact location of this village on the map, my maps were spread out on Father's table and between all of us we did some "educated" approximating on them. Fr. Cirilo told the distances to the border to the west and to the border on the north. With this information and the lay of the river, a mark was put on that section of the map that seemed to nail our location quite well.

Radio contact with the airplane was concluded. It was time to get some coffee and a bite to eat so everyone would be ready to meet the Fr. Visitor. Over coffee, I told Fr. that we would be on our way at about noon. He wanted me to stay and meet the English speaking priest; however, it was important for me to get back on the trail. Father gave me some mementos to take with me, a small basket for a girl to carry things in and a very fine-tooth nicely decorated comb—a lice comb. After coffee, good-bys were said to all and I went to the guest house to start packing.

By this time, the Papal Volunteer had returned with the tractor and trailer. After the people changed clothes and were ready, they got into the trailer according to rank and when it was loaded, they happily drove off to meet the plane. Others followed on foot making a colorful parade.

After packing, I set my gear out in the square, went back into the house and put a new roll of film in the camera. Stepping back into the square, my three guides were on hand and ready to go.

Woman with a baby pointing at the airport after the plane lands

The DC 3 came over the village and started the downwind leg for its landing. There were no more than a handful of people in the village beside the four of us. Everyone else was either at the airport or out in the field. The plane landed at the far end of the field so we could not see the touchdown or the plane until it rolled up over the rise. It taxied up to the tower and shut off the engines. In my estimation the field could handle a four engine airplane.

I made a final note in the notebook and we departed. The time was 1:30, Suriname time.

Leaving Tirio, we followed the tractor road along the river. The jungle growth made it cool, the road gave hard footing so the going was very well. The pack of supplies left by the road last night was picked up—it had not been disturbed. We continued on, meeting people as we went. They stopped to talk, asking where we were going, etc. When they learned that we were going to Alalapadu, they gave us some of their provisions and in this way some sugar cane, bananas, berries and more cassava were added to our supplies. The men had already gathered a good supply of cassava in the village, enough for this trip. The added supplies were all welcomed but really added to the load. Piri also picked up two very young, green parrots: more to carry. (I purchased one of them from him when we were in Alalapadu and carried it home with me.) About the only thing less was the beans and rice I left with the sisters.

A few kilometers north of the village, we came to a clearing that was a "business district." There was a saw mill with various wood-working tools like a power planer, power saw, hand tools and a small diesel-driven generator set, to provide power for the electric tools. Farming implements that could be attached to the Mercedes tractor were stored here. Mind you this was all in a shed, not in the open but in a shed.

This area seemed to be the center for making cement blocks. One of the first things to catch my eye when we entered Tirio was the central building made of cement blocks. The center also had a partial cement floor. One other building in Tirio made of cement blocks was the convent. Father's building was made out of lumber and sheet iron.

There was no cement mixer to be seen, either in the village or here in this clearing. Apparently it is all mixed by hand. Quite a number of blocks were curing. Just downstream from here, a rather large building was being built with blocks. There was no way of determining what this building was going to be but it will be quite large by local standards.

Sharp sand and small aggregates to about one centimeter in size were in abundance. This material was washed clean either in the river or in the savanna by the rain. Bringing in cement and mortar must be a problem. The river is not large enough to accommodate anything larger than a canoe. To the south, the river may be large enough for a small boat which could carry cement to be transshipped by canoe. If this is not possible, then the only other way is by airplane.

All of the equipment and tools were operated and maintained by the local Indians. Considering the remoteness of the area, the condition of the equipment indicated a pride as well as a degree of quality in the workmanship. There seemed to be a lot of overall enthusiasm in the work in the field as well as the mill and other work areas.

Continuing on, we met a fellow coming in from a hunt. He had an iguana and two toucans. While I was fascinated with the coloring of the birds, I was sure my boys would be interested with the weapon he was carrying. This fellow had a 22 caliber rifle with a scope. Rifles are not allowed in Suriname and of course there is no need for a scope. I took the rifle and showed my guides how to use it. They were like kids with a new toy. The scope was real new to them and it began to look as if we might be here for some time but at last we moved on.

This gave me an opportunity to put on my sandals (we had crossed a stream and I took off my footwear to keep them dry, I was wearing the sandals given to me by Fr. Cirilo) and have a closer look at the toucans.

Toucans are as incredible to look at as they are in flight. The bill is almost the same size as the body. In flight it is a mystery to see: a case of the Divine sense of humor. The bill on this particular bird looked as though an artist had cleaned his brushes out on it.

The colors were about a quarter of an inch wide, some going the length of the bill while others, near the head, were crossways—like real wild! Each one of the brush strokes was of light, almost pastel color. My guides shot a few others on the trip but none of them had the same coloration as this one. As best as I could determine, the toucans had a soft song that was only a few notes in range.

The trail for the tractor lasted a few kilometers past the saw mill, block plant. The trail continued to be good and wide with lots of signs of agriculture but fewer people. Jungle vegetation became more prominent and savanna less. This trail continued on to a group of four or five huts. Here was a woman and several children and of course some dogs. Apparently, the rest of the group was out in the fields.

We stopped here for a rest and in a few minutes the woman brought us a regular black cooking pot full of berry juice. The juice was very cool and extremely refreshing and went well with cassava bread. She brought out some extra cassava bread for us to take along. We then stepped into the jungle where we stayed for the entire journey to Alalapadu.

IV

Pousoe Tirio to Alalapadu

August 7th. (continued)

Leaving the savanna and entering the jungle, the jungle looks like an impenetrable green mass. The vegetation starts from the ground and presents a solid wall that blends into the top. Normally, the only trails are the animal tunnels. Going into this mass head-on requires using a machete to cut through. The depth of this growth depends on the type of land it is on. Where we entered the savanna yesterday, the land was very wet so heavy vegetation or bush extended for some distance. Other places, where the land was relatively dry, this growth extended in only about 30 to 40 feet until the jungle opened up. The interior of the jungle is comparable to most well-established woods: well spaced, large trees, some soft some hard wood and, in many cases, the branches started 30 to 40 feet up. The crown of the trees intermixed with each other to form a near solid canopy. Again, depending on the soil, the lower growth would be brush or stalk type.

But today, because of the nearness to the village, our trail was very clearly defined and devoid of low hanging branches. Walking was easy and progress was good. We had gone some distance when the guides came upon some monkeys. One was shot but not well enough so it was necessary for a guide to start climbing the trees to get him.

I walked down the trail a short distance to a clearing and started to set up camp. My main objective was to clear the area of Tirio that afternoon, get into the jungle and on our way. Had we waited to visit with the Father Visitor, we would have stayed overnight and thus the delay in getting on our way. We were running late and did not wish to be any later. Thus camp was set up earlier than usual.

As it turned out, it took two of the boys an hour and a half to get the monkey out of the tree. These men were actually climbing in the tree tops with a shot gun and cutlass. To say the least, this was one of the reasons for my walking down the trail to find a campsite.

One of the staples that I carried was dry beans, half were white pea beans and the other half, red beans. The people in Tirio were interested in the beans since they were not able to raise them locally. They none-the-less knew what they were and really wanted some. I left some of the red and white beans with the head sister.

By now the eating habits of the men were known to me and I was ready to do some experimenting on my own. For ease of packing and to keep the beans and rice dry, I had a few plastic bags made from what was used in the mine to bag ammonium nitrate for blasting. These bags were about three feet long and when filled would make a two and a half foot long by three and a half inch diameter container. One end was sealed with a hot iron, the other end twisted and folded over, then tied with a rubber band. In this way the beans kept dry even under water.

This evening I took a half bag or less (about a pound) and added enough water to cover the beans well. I tied the bag with a small rope and hung it in a tree, thus soaking the beans.

August 8th.

This morning started like most mornings at about 6:00. While having breakfast, coffee, tea, rice and cassava, one of the boys offered me some monkey meat. While the men always had monkey meat, they ate it by themselves and made no attempt to offer me any and I made no request. Here was an offer so I accepted. It was good but the boys like pepper and therefore it was rather peppery.

While we were having breakfast, we could hear the DC 3 that had overnighted in Tirio warm up its engines and take off. Then back to the stillness of the jungle. By 7:30 we were on our way again.

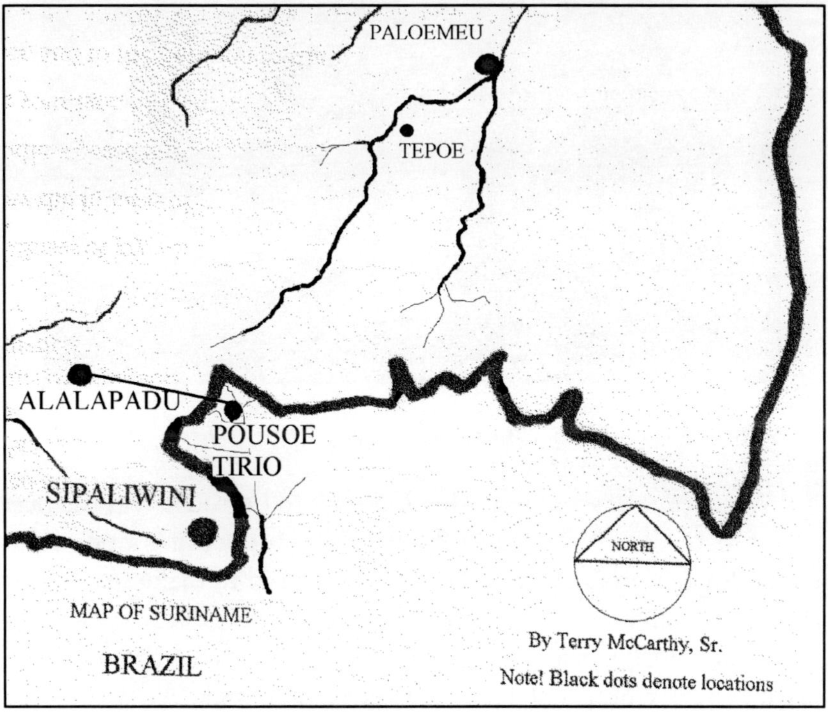

Route to Alalapadu

By 8:30 I reached the conclusion that this is where my jungle boots were going to be customized. We stopped and off came the boots and out came the knife and I proceeded to work them over. First the split was extended past the strings and down to the toe end of the boots. Next, holes were cut to allow the sore spots on either side of my foot to be free. I put the boots on and off and cut them until they fit as best they could. In planning this trip I thought it would be best to have new boots. After some time I concluded that a good old pair of worn-in boots would have been better. There had not been any rain for the past day, making walking very nice after customizing the boots.

Piri with the moetete and two parrots, starting out from camp

While progress was not what I liked it to be, today was the best day to date. We pushed on till 1:00 then stopped for a one hour break. I had a small alcohol stove that we used to make tea. While the stove enabled us to have tea or coffee on short notice, carrying it and the alcohol was a problem. In all, the stove was not worth taking and I would not take one again on a walk. As we moved on, we came to areas where it had rained so it was not too surprising when we started getting showers. It was during one of these showers that we happened to be by an old shelter so we stopped to have the above mentioned tea.

Along the way a howler monkey was shot. These are red and large and travel in a family. (In Costa Rica, Central America, they have a black monkey they called a howler but they are not like these howlers.) When one started to howl then the whole family joined in. It is something like a barking hoot, hoot, hoot, rhythm that they all join in. At night, when they are nearby, they set up a hoot that grows in volume until the entire jungle begins to shake. It is a beautiful sound. The only sound that I can think of to compare with it is a Notre Dame football game when the whole crowd starts to cheer. A family of howler monkeys can be heard miles away. This sound is very hauntingly beautiful.

Howler monkey

Storms here are something else again. We came to a clearing that had a shelter nearby. The midday sun was shining in the clearing which made it nice and warm: it had been somewhat cloudy but not much. As I sat in the sun drying off, there was a roll of thunder. The three guides moved into the shelter and set their moetetes inside. They then went out and cut a few palm branches to cover the holes in the roof. I laughed at them and said it won't rain—from the time of the first thunder until a wall of water hit us was three minutes at most. As we stood under the shelter, I remember my amusement at the sudden storm in Beethoven's Pastoral Symphony. Now, as suddenly as it started, the rain stopped—Beethoven must have been here.

On the trail itself, a shower could come on us fast; in that case the boys cut six or eight palm fronds, stood them against a small tree or sapling, three to four inches in diameter and tied them to the tree. The fronds bent over and formed a low canopy. By taking off the moetete, we stood under this canopy and kept dry. Each one of us had our own canopy. (Remember rain in the jungle comes straight down.)

Since starting this trip, I had seen these canopies along the trail and wondered what they were for. At long last I learned their use. The individual leaves were green and strong so the leaves were used as ties. Everything the Indians needed was close at hand; they learned to use everything.

While on the trail we chewed on sugar cane which was very refreshing. We took a section of the cane, cut off the outer layer and chewed on the pulp.

Depending on the weather, the shelters were built first then the fire was started or the fire was started first then the shelters were built. Either way, it was about an hour from the time we stopped until the coffee was ready. Every camp was by running water.

Today after camp was set up, I took the beans out of the plastic bag and put them in my kettle. They had been soaking for about 24 hours and were nice and puffed up. After covering them in water, I put in some salt and one or two bouillon cubes. This was put over some hot coals near the fire to start cooking. A bit of dehydrated onion from my supplies sure added to the flavor. The next addition was real far out for this particular northern dish—one large shoulder of monkey meat, cut to eating size, was added to the beans. I tried my best to keep the bean pot just at a roll, not a hard boil, but easy. Keeping some wood on the cover as a weight allowed some build-up in pressure. We had the beans ready to eat in just under an hour and a half. With cassava bread, this was as good a meal as could be found anywhere. We all enjoyed it (without pepper).

Shortly before reaching this campsite, one of the boys cut a branch or two of what looked like berries from a palm tree. (Palm trees grow in many varieties and varieties of fruit.) Each of these berries was about a half inch in diameter. The outer skin was almost like a shell and very thin. The seeds inside looked like overgrown cherry seeds. They reminded me of a concord grape of about the same size but very hard—like grapes they grew in bunches.

These berries were pulled off and put in a kettle—they sounded like marbles dropping. Water was added to cover the berries and the kettle was hung over the fire. This was left to boil a little while and then taken off the fire. By now the skins were soft. Using a stick of wood—one and a half inches around by 16 to 18 inches long with one end blunt, the boys began to pound on the berries in the pot, thus removing the skin. After some time, the seeds were removed from the kettle leaving only the water, pulp and the skins. The kettle was filled with water to the desired level and placed back over the fire. This boiled easily for a while until the skin was very soft and broken up. It was allowed to cool down somewhat. The boys brought me a cupful. It was the same kind of juice the woman gave us yesterday, not as cool, but none the less the same extremely refreshing drink. This has been a very good day, walking was at its best, the beans and monkey meat excellent and now this new found juice—a real full day. I enjoyed this camp.

As a final end to the day, there came a real "hell for leather" storm.

While we frequently had rain, there was not too much thunder. However, this night we had a real storm. The rain was a regular waterfall. The thunder was vicious and most of it was the sharp whip-crack type. When the thunder rolled in, it came as a steady roll until it was upon us then the roll was punctuated by very sharp cracks until it rolled off—at its height everything shook. The most unusual part of this storm was the lightning—it was visible only in the immediate area. Thus at least 75% of the thunder was preceded by darkness. The final explosion was like a large dynamite blast—there was no flash only the blast preceded by a hiss, or as a crackle, that made one take notice: then the shock wave. All of this, the crackle, shock wave and the explosion were almost as one and were so intense I fully expected a shower of debris to hit—then the smell of lighting when it comes close.

This was the final explosion and the storm rolled away very reluctantly until it lost itself off toward the Amazon: then only the sound of rain. Quite an experience in a jungle hammock

Sunday August 9.

After a good night's sleep, I woke up to find the rain had stopped but the jungle was dripping. The river, Kamariwini, was about two feet higher than last night so we obviously had a good rain over the general area. I went to check the charts because the boys named the river—I left those charts back in Tirio. The charts I have are west of the border. This river, Tirio, and the fact that we moved WNW all day were my only indicators of our location.

The boys were in no hurry to move so I had coffee. They read from their note books and sang some of their songs. This was their Sunday service. I said most of my Liturgical Prayer. This marks one week on the trail, last Sunday we left Sipaliwini. They made some more berry juice and tea.

We left camp about 9:00 and 15 minutes later came to a river crossing. With the high water this was a real problem. Between nine and 11 we traveled one hour and spent one hour crossing streams. At the first crossing, I cut a pole to use when walking on the log crossing. The pole was about 12 feet long but it took a 15 footer to reach bottom. As I started across, I said to myself, "ole man, you are going to get your ass wet today".

Sometimes high water flooded large flat areas: at these points I took my boots off and walked barefoot. At noon we came to a stream crossing that showed a very definite sign the water had dropped. This was good news because we were moving uphill and thus less water ahead. Progress was very slow and ole dad did get his ass wet.

By 2:30 we arrived at a place where all the ridges pulled together. This left us no choice but to go head-on into the hills. The slope was about 1:1 but was mostly coarse sand with enough vegetation to give some footing, however, still damn near straight up. It took an hour of huff and puff to get to the top. This leveled out for a while then back down a very sharp but not too deep drop. We reached the bottom at 4:00 which was no wider than 50 feet, then back up the next equally sharp hill. After another hour of huff and puff, we topped this ridge. At the very top of the ridge stood a giant tree all by itself in a relatively clear area. I stopped to admire this giant commanding this hill.

We topped the ridge and started going down another ridge that fell off sharply on both sides. A very clearly defined trail, about five feet wide ran down the ridge. We were back in Suriname.

After moving down the ridge for a short while, I heard rushing water to the left some distance ahead. By the sound, we were paralleling the water but then we ran out of ridge and had to go down off the slope. Unlike the other side we just came up, this side was steeper with big boulders, practically no small vegetation, some trees and the soil very fine. On top of all this, everything was wet. The only good thing about this slope was that we were going down. Had it been a little worse, I would have used a rope.

When we got to the bottom of the slope by the stream, I stopped to take some pictures. This boulder-strewn stream bed was really a canyon. To film the top of the stream to where we were standing, took two frames. Turning around, I shot a picture of the lower part. I estimated we were midway down this canyon.

The two younger men went ahead and were already working on the camp site when I arrived about 5:30. We made camp later than usual. It was not a good site but the best in the area. It was getting dark fast and well after dark when I finished washing my clothes. The guides had eaten so when I arrived they handed me a plate with rice, parrot and cassava.

Earlier, at about noon, as we walked along a hillside, one of the boys saw a macaw sitting in a palm tree eating berries. The fellow pointed to the bird and gave me the shotgun. This was the only time they offered me the gun to shoot. The tree was down hill from us and the red, green, yellow and blue macaw was in the top so the shot was very nearly level–now I was eating macaw. The body looked like a duck's body. As usual, the boys gave it a shot of pepper so I can only say it tasted like peppery chicken.

When we arrived at a camp site, the guides' usual procedure was to take off their moetete and loin cloth and go into the creek or river and splash off for a while. If need be, they took this opportunity to defecate also. They carried pants and shirts in the moetete—when we were in the savanna they put them on. However, in the jungle they preferred the loin cloth. When approaching a village they put on a fresh red one—in the jungle they wore faded and shorter ones. When needed they would tear off a piece of the loin cloth and use the strip to tie something. As a result the loin cloth had a number of uses. The loin cloths were about six feet long and a foot and a half wide. With a band around their waist, the loin cloth went over the band in front then between their legs and over the band in back.

August 10.

It started to rain about 2:00AM and continued the rest of the night. Something I could never quite understand was that if we made camp when it was raining, the fire was built under the shelter, if it was not raining the fire was built outside. Last night it was not raining so the fire was outside, needless to say, the fire was drowned out. The clothes hung by the fire to dry, including my boots were rather wet also. The boys started a fire but it was some time before my boots were dry.

Our camp was by the stream we had been following through the canyon. When we moved out we continued on downstream. The general area had many boulders and after going about a mile, the stream was lost into some boulders and that was the last we saw of it until about a half mile later when it came out from under this great pile of boulders. We could hear it most of the time while it was in that pile of rocks.

The water had risen during the night and was flowing much faster. The boys started cutting trees, about 18" to 24" through, with their cutlass. Even at that size it took about six of them before they had one big and long enough to stay—the other ones would hit the water and be washed away. The tree that stayed was about six to eight inches underwater in midstream—the time was about 8:15.

We were about two days late so we decided to send Pori with a message to Claude at Alalapadu to let him know when to expect us. Pori departed at 9:15 and Yanamore, Piri and I left camp by 10:00. The creek was a roaring river about ten feet deep. I finished roll No. two and started roll No. three in the camera. Sometime later, I took my boots off and waded through a rather low spot. It was of course, necessary for me to dry and service my feet after each crossing. Each time we reached a stream that I could not jump, there was usually a tree or some branches to walk on. The boys usually made a bridge with anything from a small tree on up: this made for slow progress. A little detour around a puddle takes extra time.

Everywhere were birds of every color, description and song. One bird I never did meet face to face was trying a theme from Stravinsky's Firebird Suite. It was able to do a beautiful job over the first five or six notes then either forgot the music or became so overwhelmed by the beauty of the first notes that it was over-emotional and could not go on. At any rate, it crapped out every time.

Another bird I never saw but heard came off like the aged soprano found in most Church choirs. A part of its song was fairly well defined but rather raggy. Then it reached for a high note and cracked up every time. A pause followed and then, as if encouraged by some well-wishers, started all over again. This failed attempt at a comeback made me at least grin but not laugh because it always reminded me of the parish choirs I had known, with the old worn-out sopranos who were kept on and on and on and etc., etc.

The first two days of travel out of Tirio, were relatively dry and we made very steady progress. We were now getting a considerable amount of rain and with the high water were loosing time—we had to push to make the regular camp site that the men used when in that area. (My progress was slow, so I had to push myself and not the guides.)

Drying monkey meat on a rack built over a fire

During the day, the boys shot a bird that looked like a grouse. Somewhat later they shot a monkey. Piri was the first at the camp and found some monkeys there. He took the gun and went off through the bush and shot two of them. Yano shot another one so we had four monkeys and a bird. One of the monkeys was a female with a baby. The baby was not hurt so they brought it in with the mother. They asked me if I wanted the monkey and I said NO. In the process of trying to kill the baby, Piri threw it down hard on the ground several times. After a while, it started to cry so he tried to strangle it. This went on for about 10 minutes—so I stepped over and took the little fellow and showed them how to do the job properly. I took the little monkey by the legs and tail, swung him way back and then forward, slamming the back of his head hard against a tree and that was the end of him.

In general, this was a good camp. We had a nice log fire so most of my cloths got dry. I moved in close to the fire and in a while I was dry and warm, the first time in about three days.

Processing monkey seems to be the same all the time. Some of the parts are cooked but the body is smoked and dried. The fur is removed from the hide by using hot water to loosen it up, much like scalding and scraping a hog. They are not skinned. The animal is cut into the desired pieces. A good fire is built and a wooden rack is placed over it, the meat is put on the rack. The fire is kept going all night so by morning the meat is smoked and dried. We ate what was shot but the boys never had more than a day's supply ahead. However, when coming into a village (Pousoe Tirio, Alalapadu and later Tepoe), we picked up extra game to take into the village with us, especially to their homes.

August 12.

We had a very good night and I slept well. However, at 6:15 the rain started so we stayed in camp until about 10:00 then moved out. Progress was good but a little wet. At 1:30 we came to very beautiful rapids. Pori had made camp here last night so he should be in Alalapadu by now.

Rapids are not clear; decomposing vegetation colors the water

The boys splashed in the cool water and got cooled off. We stayed and rested for a while and then started off. The rapids were rather wide and somewhat deep where we crossed: fortunately, a large tree had fallen across the stream so we walked over on it. On one of the crossings a nest of wasps near the tree on which we crossed, concerned the boys very much. They took extra care in getting me by them. They must have been very bad bugs. We camped at 6:00 some distance from water, but it was a nice camp.

At some point along here we stopped and picked up a bundle of arrowcane. The guides cut and bundled them on their trip to meet me at Sipaliwini. Arrowcane grows straight and smooth and is used to make arrows. The arrows are about six feet long and by nature are very straight and smooth. (Regular cane has joints at intervals and is not very straight.) The tip is placed on the heavy end and the feathers on the smaller end.

A bundle of arrowcane (upper right) and toucans

There seems to be three basic types of tips on the arrows. One type is a blade: some large, others small. Another tip was barbed about 10 inches long and narrow with about 10 barbs. The barbed tip was used on fish. The third type is the poisoned tip: curare.

(Curare is an extract of a vine these Indians use, that produces muscular relaxation) The tip of the arrow shaft is made so the poison tips can be inserted into the end. There is no poisoned tip installed while carrying these arrows, they are installed only when they are ready to be used. This bundle of arrowcane was carried back to Alalapadu.

Most of the time while in the jungle, everything smelled clean. After a rain everything smelled scrubbed clean. In the savanna, there was usually the hot dry smell. We did not spend much time in the savanna nor did we camp there so I did not get acquainted with any special smells there.

Smells came on the breeze and it was possible for them to carry over for some distance. A number of times the heavy smell of blossoms would come, heavy as lemon blossom, thick as syrup, and completely surrounding us even though there was no great or extra ordinary amount of flowers in the area.

At times a brief pleasing scent would be there, yet not—just a hint or suggestion of a perfume—like that of a woman who knows how to use good perfume.

There was an occasional smell of fermentation, the sweet smell not the dry musty smell. I do not recall ever smelling decaying flesh at any place or time on the trip.

The smell of smoke was the most difficult to get accustomed to. The wood used for camp fire was a special type that had a very bitter, biting smell. At first, it almost made me sick. It was the smell I first noticed when I met the Indians: a smell that I never became fond of even though I later became accustomed to and was not bothered by it any more. No doubt I smelled from this smoke when I returned home.

August 13.

This morning the boys spent some time getting trimmed up. These men are tough as nails and it seemed odd for them to trim themselves. They took tweezers and plucked all the hair on their face, including their eye brows. (Note page #16) Depending on their hair style, some shaved in front of their ears. They usually combed their hair with bangs with the rest of the hair pulled back and wrapped with a heavy string in a pig tail. Sometimes they would pull the pig tail through a piece of bamboo.

Beads were wrapped around the legs and arms. I was told this is a sign of their wealth. All of this took an extra 45 minutes so I knew we must be getting close to some place. Shortly after starting out, we met two men on their way to Tirio. We stopped and exchanged greetings, then moved on. We later met two more men. One was the father of Piri. He obviously had a better sense of humor than his son who had a real good one. The only real indication of getting closer to a village was that the trail was becoming very well defined. There were fields of various sizes in varying stages of cultivation. The fields were not concentrated near the village but rather indiscriminately cut out of the jungle.

Walking through these fields was of course in the open and therefore hot from the sun. However, a very slight breeze carried the cool air from the jungle and oddly enough gave a chilling effect. Then, with the abruptness of the jungle and the savanna, we were in Alalapadu. The overall vegetation was too dense to see any distance ahead so entering the village was like opening a door, there it was: Alalapadu at 12:05.

V

Mission Alalapadu

August 13 (cont.)

The mission Alalapadu, like Tirio, is located on a hill by a river. I do not know the name of this river but it flows southwest into the Sipaliwini River. Drinking water is taken in from the upper part of the river where it enters the village. Downstream they wash their clothes. Further down, the women and children bathe, still further down, the men and boys bathe. Where the river exits the village is the swimming pool. Claude and his wife were not at the mission when I arrived. Two of their sons, Marie Heritage an American woman, and a nurse from Holland greeted me.

After settling in a bit, I took my trusty Pentax and started on a tour of the town. The camera provided two reactions: the younger kids were quite interested and wanted their pictures taken, older people, from their 20s on up, stepped out of sight if given the opportunity. If they were occupied, there was no attempt to have their picture taken or to move out of sight. The people of Alalapadu have the open simplicity of those who know the wonders of the modern world but are satisfied with what they have.

A very basic philosophy among the Indians is quite simple: if an Indian is making something, it is because he needs it, if the need is not there, it will not be made. Fortunately, several people at the time were in need of things so the camera did find something worthwhile.

Putting the finishing touches on a bow

Tying feathers on an arrow

One man was putting the finishing touches on a six foot long bow. The wood was very straight-grained hardwood. His tool was the lower jaw of a wild pig: this tusk is strong and sharp. By drawing the tusk over the wood, nice shavings were dropping off, bringing the wood down to exactly what he wanted. He was sitting in front of his house—when I approached, he kept working. His wife, however, thought this was very funny: she sat by the door of the house laughing. The bow I later purchased was made from a wood called leatherwood.

Another man was making an arrow—he was tying the feathers on it. I wondered if he was using some of the arrowcane we brought in with us.

Some women were making cassava bread—the cassava root is one of the staples in this country and many other countries as well (oddly the juice is poisonous). When living as nomads, these people harvested their cassava wherever they found it. Now, adapting to stationary-type living, they plant it quite extensively. The root is cleaned and grated to a fine pulp. This pulp is then placed in a squeezer to remove as much of the poisonous juice as possible.

The cassava squeezer is made from wood fibers and woven into a long cylinder as a regular basket weave. When stretched out, it is four feet long and three inches in diameter. On each end of this cylinder, a loop is woven as a part of the squeezer, top and bottom. By compressing the cylinder, end to end, the action of the weave will expand the diameter of the cylinder to five inches, almost double, and reduce its length to about three feet.

The loop at the open end of the cylinder is hooked or tied to a tree branch or a stub five to six feet high. The compressed squeezer is filled with cassava pulp. When it is full, a pole is put through the lower loop. The lower or short end of the pole is put under a root or some other object. The operator then takes the longer end of the pole and begins to bring it down. This stretches the cylinder and at the same time the weave contracts the diameter of the cylinder and squeezes the juice out of the cassava pulp. By repacking and squeezing, the mass becomes very compacted and dry. Someone once told me the cassava squeezer is like the constrictor snake.

I am not sure what the complete process is but in the final stages, the cassava is formed into a large pancake about two feet in diameter and a half inch thick. This is fried over a big fire. When taken off the frying pan, it is very hard and dry. These are then placed on the roof of the house to super-dry in the sun and become harder—from a distance they look like a bunch of white manhole covers lying on the roof. When super-dried, the cassava cakes are edible for a long time. While traveling, they are very light and can be broken up into smaller pieces and easily carried in the moetete.

Cassava bread (left) drying on the roof of a hut

(In a recent issue of the magazine, "Jesuits and Friends" is an article about a Jesuit missionary in Guyana in the early 1900s. He said the Amerindians at his time asked if there will be cassava in heaven. Cassava was and is a staple for these people: no wonder they asked if there would be cassava in heaven.)

Macaw parrots are kept in all the villages as pets as well as for food. They had a string around a leg and attached to a post. Scientists are studying the parrots hoping to find a way to increase their production of eggs: thus the parrots could be used like chickens as a source of food.

Continuing on my walk, I found one woman spinning string from some floss. This floss is gathered and processed and spun into string for various uses. The woman's daughter was using it to string beads. The bead colors were basic blue, red and white in color. These people seem to favor the red and blue beads. Strands are 20 feet long—these are wrapped around the lower legs or arms and around the neck.

Beads woven into belts or head bands are usually sold.—those for selling had some green or yellow beads in the pattern. This spun string seems to be very strong and was used quite extensively.

One of the real fringe benefits of this village was Steve Leavitt, Claude Leavitt's son. While around, he was able to answer some of my questions. Steve also helped me get set up in his ma and dad's house. It was nice to be set up like this so I could find the place in the dark.

Group photo in Alalapadu, following church services

In the late afternoon there was some activity going on at the church. Later, I found that Thursday evening was men's night at church. When the service was over, it was obvious that a good number of the village men had attended, older teenage boys were included. Marie Heritage told me that one evening a week was for men and one evening for the women. The people have their own elders and conduct their own Christian services. Each person had a notebook, and wrote in his own language the various bible passages, etc.: they can read these privately or in community. The religious meetings were held to discuss the Bible—it also helped them learn to read and write their own language.

Marie Heritage was an elderly woman whose husband had died. He had been a minister so when he passed away, she decided after retirement to become a missionary in this village. There was also a younger woman here from Holland who was a nurse. She spoke very good English. She usually had an Indian baby girl with her. She told me that the mother died and she had "unofficially" adopted the baby. I asked her to do some First Aid on my feet.

She was a nurse from Holland and had a clinic building there which was a standard for these missions. Each one was white and stood out amid the thatched houses of the locals. The MAF (Missionary Aviation Fellowship) pilots told me these clinic buildings were all precut to fit into the 206 Cessna they were flying. They brought them into the missions and assembled the buildings on site

The white building in the center is the local clinic

Before it became dark, there was one thing that needed to be taken care of. I had not been in town very long when I found a real sit-down "john". Unlike the monster at Tirio, this one was a real comfort station. The building was more than adequate but the openings provided more than cross ventilation. This place was so complete that it was even equipped with a stack of reading material. While some "regularity" had been established since Tirio, it was worth another visit if for no other reason than to catch up on my reading.

Ten years ago (1960 to 1970), these Indians had only a spoken language. When Claude Leavitt arrived, he reduced the sounds to written sounds with the meaning of the words in this area of the Guyana's. This was Claude's primary work for the Foreign Language Institute. He had a small ditto machine and turned out a number of printed sheets of the translation for use by various persons.

Once the people could read and write their native language, they began to learn the official language of the country which in this case was Dutch. Occasionally, the Indians used a word or two in Dutch. Claude provided me with a phonics alphabet and a list of words and phrases with English equivalent.

The mission at Pousoe Tirio was in existence longer than Alalapadu so the people there were almost bilingual—their native language and Portuguese, the second language.

An evening meal was a regular Paramaribo meal which I enjoyed along with Mrs. Marie Heritage and some others. Then the evening activities began. The house was more than a place to live—it was a general meeting place.

I was introduced to the three men who would take me on the next part of the trip to the Tapanahoni River. Through an interpreter I conveyed to them when I needed to be at the Tapanahoni—the time and location had to coincide with the canoe sent up to meet me.

The first group explained to the new group that I was not a fast traveler and needed to take a rest after climbing the big hills. To me this was very amusing. These people are very open, but more so is the innocence of their openness. It was good for a few good laughs by everyone. Being the subject of the joke, I enjoyed it very much.

At the time of this visit, the idea of a money economy was just beginning to be seen. These people had no real idea of value—the missionaries determined the value of things. One could say one, five or ten Guilders (the name of the Dutch currency) and there would not be any real correlation between the object and the monitory value. There was no concept of multiplying, etc. Basically, the guides knew how much per day they were getting but when multiplying by the number of days it lost all significance. After calculating the amount to be paid, I made three piles of money. Each pile was made up of different denominations of bills. The missionaries said that each pile was equal and correct. So the men took the money at their word. The three men who were my guides and companions were paid for their time: beginning when they left Alalapadu two weeks before.

Once the people found out that money was going about, a number of items came out to be sold, traded or swapped. The items offered were from new to old and used ones. I was short of funds so a "line of credit" was established. Additional money would be sent by way of the MAF when I returned to Paramaribo. With that, we got to work.

In the end, I acquired two bows, seven arrows, three flutes, one pair of anteater claws, one pair of nose feathers (bird tail feathers, worn in their pierced nose), one set of arm feathers (parrot feathers stuck in the arm band), and one green parrot. Between what I was able to pay, there remained a bill of 49 Guilders.

August 14,
Rosemary's birthday

The Leavitt's had a nice bed—I had a good night's sleep. There was plenty of good food to eat at breakfast so I started this leg of the journey well fed. I wrote a note to my wife and the kids, packed up three rolls of exposed film to be sent to Paramaribo by the next MAF flight along with the bows, arrows, flutes, etc.

We all had quite a time of packing and repacking and getting things ready to go. A large amount of cassava was included because there were no villages on the way and the men also needed cassava for their return trip.

Amid a large crowd we were off just after 7:30 for the next part of the journey. Walking east we passed the "airport". A rather large shed was used to store barrels for gas and the normal supplies and things used at the field.

The landing strip was basically an area cleared of brush and trees. The strip runs over the general lay of the land and there is little evidence of excavation or fills to make the field level. After looking at the field, I could easily understand the remark Neil Biddle, the head pilot for MAF, made: he said that every new MAF pilot flying out of Paramaribo must make a number of landings and takeoffs from each of these fields with a local MAF pilot before they were allowed to fly solo. Neil said that included all pilots regardless of how many hours of flying they had logged: that seemed like a good requirement.

Alalapadu with the runway from the airplane

About a half an hour out, I could hear some boys hollering in back of us. Shortly, Steve and a few of his friends came running up—I had forgotten to leave the key for their house. I agreed with Steve that it made more sense for him to have the key instead of me. With that Steve left and we continued on.

There had not been any rainfall the previous day but everything was wet from the dew. Between the grass, weeds, cassava, young banana trees and other small trees, we were all soaked in a short time. It seemed odd to have a clear sky with sun shining and be completely soaked at the same time.

At 8:30 we made our first stop. Away from the activities of the village, we thought it a good idea to take a nose count and be sure who we all were. Two young men, an older man about my age, his little son, three dogs and a parrot comprised the group.

As a part of the routine we were getting into, I decided to stop for a five to ten minute break every hour. By 9:00 we were out of the farm areas of Alalapadu and back into the jungle.

VI

Alalapadu to Tapanahoni River

August 14 (cont)

Traveling was beautiful and it was relatively dry and cool. By 10:00 we stopped for a break and took an inventory. We had a new crew: A young fellow, Sikaminan, who I called "the wise one", another young fellow, Santana, was very quiet and just carried his load. The third one was an older man about my age, Surenke, and his son Tomas—the son was about six or eight I called him "Little Beaver", a name of a little Indian boy in a comic strip.

The older man and his son carried bows and arrows. The son had a kid-size bow, arrows and moetete—they carried the bows and arrows by hand, no such thing as a quiver for the arrows, the three dogs and parrot: quite a crew.

Going was good and we continued on at a good pace. At 1:30 it started to rain and from then on it rained on and off. There were some dry spots, some wet spots like most previous days. Arrived at our camp site at 3:30 and set up camp. A bird was shot and cooked which we had with cassava. I saw my first snake today.

This was a nice established camp a short distance from a stream. We had the usual settling in. This evening the moon was shining and lit up the camp: a beautiful clear evening, great to be out here. The night sounds took over and sent us off to sleep.

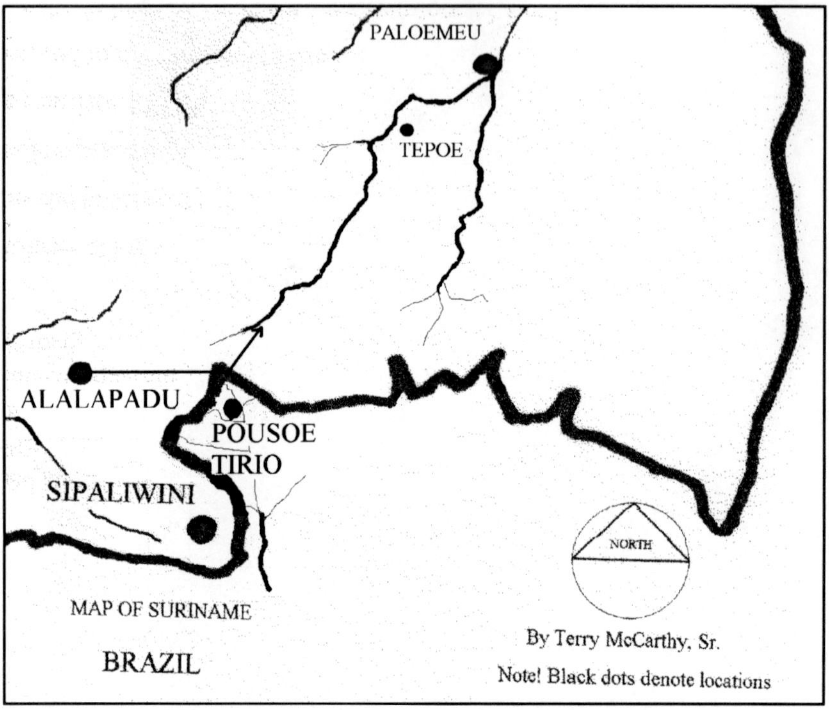

Route from Alalapadu to Tapanahoni River

Saturday, August 15.

We left camp at 7:15, traveling was very good so no stops until 9:00. It has not rained and my feet were dry. This is the best I have felt so far. We came to a rapids and I took some photos. One of the boys shot a monkey in a tree and it became hung up so they took the axe and chopped down the tree. Unknown to them they had shot a second monkeys in that tree. The tree was about 20" where it was cut, and about 50' high before the branches started. It took them about an hour in total to accomplish this and recover the two monkeys and then on our way again. Quite unlike the other crew, who climbed the tree with their shot gun and cutlass to get the monkey— cutting the tree down seems much safer. We also got a turkey (oko) and I saw my second snake, green and two and a half feet long.

We were now in some steep hills. I don't know if these are the worst or not. I am reminded of a complaint one of these boys made, the wise one, before we left Alalapadu—"if we stopped at the top of each hill, this trip could take a long time". On these big hills, he was always the happiest one to stop. The boys were very good, as good as the other crew. It was a hard day but beautiful and dry. About 2:30 we saw a small boa about six or seven feet long.

We arrived at the camp site at 3:30, right on target, again an established camp. Heading south and west, we were presently by the Itolu River. It may seem that we were wandering again, this was not the case—our general direction was North and East.

Sunday August 16

The boys started their prayer service about 5:30. We moved out at 7:30 and so far it looks like another beautiful day. We followed the Itolu River until it joined the Acalope River about 2:30. In the AM, we were moving south and west but by late afternoon we were moving west by north.

Everyone was worn out including the dogs. Every time we stopped, the dogs went to sleep and were the last ones to move out. The little boy was a tough nut—he was with us all the way.

At camp, one of the dogs went to sleep and when the old man threw it some cassava bread, it didn't even wake up. About twenty minutes later it woke and ate the bread.

Little Beaver had some arrows that had a knot from a tree branch where three or four branches grew out for a tip. (These branches were cut off short.) The shank was about ½ inch in diameter and went into the arrow shaft. This particular tip is used to stun an animal. Little Beaver would shoot at small birds—he hit some, some he missed. Good practice.

Streams and crossings and other areas begin to look alike. We set up camp near a swamp area. The camp had to be built but it was a good camp. We found a turtle here, good eating.

Monday August 17

Clear, no rain, looks good. The boys started their prayer service about 5:00. I got up at 6:30 and we were off by 7:45.

About 9:30, we came to an old camp (Acolope River head?) with a good stream. The boys said there would be no more water for about four hours so they prepared to take a rest and water down.

The old man took his bow and arrows and went after some macaws. He let fly an arrow and hit one in the tail section. The old bird came out of the tree, got himself started and flew past us about head high, chattering like hell with the arrow shaft hanging out of his tail. He flew into some brush and came out the other end without the arrow. He came around toward us and sat in a tree overhead and proceeded to give everybody hell. By the time the old man got another arrow ready and was ready to shoot, the parrot went further away with his foul language. We did not recover the arrow. The score: minus one macaw and one arrow. We saw some monkeys but the boys did not want to shoot them.

After about an hour of R & R, I filled the canteen and we started up a hill. It was head-on till about 11:30. Through the jungle, we saw we were on one of the more prominent hills. To the north and a bit east it was relatively wide open, to the south was a hill higher than we were. Continuing east, we finally came to water at about 2:00—three and a half hours from our last water.

The boys said it was the Perue (or Paru) Creek—this would be the head waters of the river that runs through Missao Pousoe Tirio—Brazil again. We made camp at 3:30, a nice location and an old camp. The boys promptly shot a monkey and went out after another. Two monkeys tonight, one has long black hair and I would say stands three feet tall.

As we approached the Tapanahoni, there were flocks of macaws all over the jungle: they're noisy as hell, especially in the morning and evening, during the day they let you know they are there—never any question as to whether there are macaws in the area. At this camp, a flock of them landed in the tree canopy above us. They began chewing on twigs and branches so there was now a constant shower of twigs, leaves, nuts or shells (and other ornaments) showering to the ground below. Macaws are very beautiful in the trees or in flight. They always fly in pairs, one ahead of the other and to one side, but they are sure short on music. We had a good hard day. I am doing better every day but my feet are still giving me problems—still not what I would like to be doing.

Previously I mentioned the howler monkeys. These are red in color and travel in a family. At night the family will start to howl. One starts then the whole family will joins in. When they are nearby, the jungle will shake, it becomes a roar. A family of howler monkeys can be heard miles away. I learned to enjoy the sound, it is a very hauntingly beautiful sound.

August 18

The weather has had a lot to do with our progress on this part of the trip. We have made good time and made our target camps by 3:30. This gives us an easy afternoon and helps us get an early start in the AM. We were up and out at 7:45. I felt that everyone was in the best shape. I felt good and was sure I could push myself.

During the morning, the older man, Surenke, had a chance to use his poison tip arrow on a monkey. The poison tip is a strip of bamboo that can be four or five inches long, 3/8 to ½ inches wide, and about 1/8 inch thick. These tips are dipped in curare and then left to dry. The tips look like they have been painted brown when the poison is dried. On trips like this, these tips were carried in a section of bamboo about six inches long. This bamboo is hollowed out and a leather cap is put on the top. In this way, they can carry 10 to 15 extra poison tips.

. The arrow shaft is standard length but the end is made special to receive the blunt end of the poison tip. When they are ready to use, the tip is notched all around just below the poison line. This is done so when the tip penetrates the game and stops, the weight of the shaft will break the tip off at the notch leaving the poison tip in the animal. I would imagine that if it were otherwise, the monkey could pull the tip out. It took the monkey about ten minutes to relax, let go and fall out of the tree.

As usual, because of the dense growth, I could not see all the action but I sure did hear it all. There was the twang of the bow string, the swish of the arrow as it went through some leaves then a good solid thump as the arrow hit home, the grunt of the monkey and his subsequent hollering then the noise of the arrow shaft falling back to the ground. The distance was some 50 to 60 feet straight up. Each sound was fairly clear by itself, twang, swish, thump and the combined noises after. My mind did a flash-back of not too many years ago when men were shot this way.

Monkey killed by poison tip, which broke off in his chest

At about noon, Sikaminan pointed out a place just off the trail where a timber monument stood. It was about eight inches by eight inches square and five feet high and was pointed at the top. It was on the crest of a ridge: the continental divide. They said this was the border between Suriname and Brazil. Took some pictures and looked for a concrete bench mark but the post was all there was.

Continental divide between Suriname and Brazil

At 12:30, we crossed a very small stream and the boys said it was the start of the Tapanahoni River.

At 1:30, we hit some hills head on; two of them were real bastards. They were high and vertical. When we came off the second one I called a stop. The boys said we had to go on to make our target camp. We were all tired and as for myself, I had reached my full extent and was not going any further, just now. This was the only time during the walk that I reached my limit but here it was. We rested for a while then moved on.

At 4:00 we hit a real nice campsite so I told the boys we would camp here. This was not our target camp but everyone was tired and I had reached my full extent, so we made camp: it was a good camp.

It had a very nice stream and I really enjoyed taking a bath and washing some clothes. There was a lot of grass here which was rather unusual.

August 19

We moved out at 7:45 and right into some hills, real bastards, but they are the last ones. Back in Alalapadu, there had been mention of three big hills—this must be hill number three. Things in general leveled out but there were still some sharp but thankfully low hills.

We came to a large stream with some nice fish swimming in it. The old man using an arrow with a broad blade tip, shot at two of them and got one. These fish were anjoemara—a throwback to the prehistoric period—with its wicked set of teeth and fighting spirit. It was one of the best, if not the best tasting fish—but they are damn ornery.

Guide retrieving arrow and fish

We approached and passed a flat depression and I heard a bird's song for the first and only time. The men said it was a bird but we never saw this one. Its song was about seven or eight notes long.

Each tone was clear, full, exact and rich. The song bounced all over and each note would be sharp, flat or a "blue note". While I am a very good whistler, I could not get the pattern, only a tape recorder could have captured this song. After being in the jungle for a period of time, hearing this for the first time, I stopped and listened for a while. At the time, I wished I had a tape recorder so I could tape it and send it to Stan Kenton. It would have been interesting to hear what he would do with such a group of notes.

Progress was good and we arrived at the Tapanahoni at 5:15. There was no one there to meet us but then we didn't expect them to be. We were on a tributary called Kimni by the Bush Negro and Pitoli by the Trios. The Tapanahoni is about 100 yards past our camp. We had a real good day and the beans and fish were ready by 8:30, we all enjoyed this good meal.

The water in the jungle is not clear but has a brown tint to it. It is called Coca Cola water. The dead vegetation on the jungle floor is decomposing. The water from the rain absorbs some of the coloration or dye from this material. The water is good to drink—at least I had no ill effects from drinking it.

This was an old established camp but not very big. We were able to get set up very easily and just sit back and enjoy. Some red ants moved in so we needed to clean up and get rid of them—"Sevin" did help.

August 20

We did nothing today. The boys went fishing and tied into a big one about two and a half feet long but he snapped the line easily. Other than that we did nothing but some map reading, used the compass and then some language work, all of which was interesting

The Suralco boat arrived at 3:30 with five men on board. (From the Geological Dept) They had a box for me with the items I asked my wife to send. I was able to pay the men for their time from Alalapadu and back—also paid "Little Beaver" something.

Guides and I at end of walk

We had sick call that evening and patched up some cuts on the guides. They didn't like the iodine too well but liked the big patch. One of them who came on the boat had knocked a toe nail off completely so I bandaged that toe.

Ma sent a letter with the box so I enjoyed reading it. It was dated August 5, 1970. Terry also sent a letter. Ma said they had celebrated Kevin's birthday with a chocolate cake and ice cream. She also said when they sang happy birthday to Kevin, Flint, our macaw, sang along with them. Both Terry and Ma commented on Terry having problems with his English course. He told Ma he thought he was loosing it—when waking up that morning he thought to himself, "Me thinks I shalt arise now". Kevin told Ma that he thought of me every time he had a cold beer, at his old age. Every one sent hugs and kisses.

We ended our journey together with a swap session. I was able to swap my 100 feet of nylon rope for a bow, two arrows and a bamboo container with poison tips—time to call it a day, also the end of the walk, and get into the hammock.

VII

River Trip

August 21

Camp started waking up at the usual time. We had breakfast and began moving gear to the boat. I found a scorpion under the box, the first one on the trip. The family must have sent it to me from Paramaribo—just another gift from home.

The guides from Alalapadu said their prayers, sang some of their songs and gave us their blessing. I, in turn, gave them my blessing. We pushed off at 7:45 for our trip downriver, the others started on their return to Alalapadu.

The boat they sent was a dugout about 20 to 25 feet long, made out of a single log, with extra sideboards running the length of the boat. It was about two and a half feet deep and three to three and a half feet wide in the center. It was completely loaded, not with just my things but with all the supplies for the boat and the crew including an extra outboard motor, about five HP, and gasoline for the motors.

The five-man crew consisted of two men in the bow: one, Itapoe, standing as the lookout, gave signals to the man in back with the motor. I called the motor man, Piesolie, the Captain. Itapoe had a long pole to push us off boulders or push tree branches out of the way. The other man sitting up front with a paddle to help direct the bow was Pisi. Most of the gear was stored behind the two lookouts. Two more men, the youngest, Anasinka, the other was Pareya (who had the toe nail broken off—I called him "sore toe"). My seat, a board, which had no give to it except my butt, was next in line. Behind me was the Captain with the motor.

This was a good crew. They all knew what to do. The only problem I had was the board seat: the boat was round bottom so I had to sit like a statue, no movements. The seats were fastened directly to the top of the main log and were a low part of the structure. After being on my feet for so long, sitting was very nice—for a while—after a while it was like riding a picket fence. The guides all had excellent balance and could move around like cats. I was like an elephant along for the ride.

The Captain, Piesolie, was recommended very highly by all who knew him. The other men did what he said. He did things with that boat I never expected could be done with a dugout. All five of them had been employed by Suralco to work with the Geological Department and had worked as a team before.

During the night some trees and branches had fallen in the river so we had trees to cut and move around. This ride was fantastic. The head lookout gave a hand signal and the skipper twisted and bent the boat around boulders or logs that were under the water. If the lookout thought the tree across the river was low enough, the skipper cranked up the motor and over the log we went. One time we tried going over a tree that was about eight to 10 inches out of the water. We didn't get all the way over and had to get out and strong-arm the boat the rest of the way over.

As we moved along, small streams came in from either side. This widened the river. The earlier part of the trip, where the river was narrow, presented the most tree problems; if the tree was high enough we went under. Then we came to a large tree we could not go over or under so we stopped and the guides cut it in half. The largest of these trees took about 45 minutes.

Prior to 10:00, a lot of boulders and trees slowed us up. I mentioned earlier that we were in the start of the dry season. By the water line on some boulders, the water was three to four feet lower than usual. That made the flow slower with more trees and boulders exposed. The river twists and turns—the jungle is a wall of green at the river's edge: like going down a canyon. We were in and out of the sun: the sun was hot but it was very cool in the shade. Taking photos was difficult in the extreme change of light. I used the Spotmatic all the time enabling me to make minor adjustments. Looking downstream, I anticipated general settings and then fine-tuned the setting at the time I took the photo.

After 10:00, the river was wide and smooth enough that the motor was shut off and the men went fishing. We drifted for an hour and they caught about 10 nice pan-size fish. This fishing experience was wild. They had short sticks or poles with the line tied on the end. It was heavy line with a steel leader on the hook end: few feet of line possibly eight to 10 feet long. The men wound up and swung the business end (the hook) around throwing it as far out as possible: these big hooks were flying just overhead—I looked for a hole to crawl into. Fortunately, no one got a hook in the head or body.

When not fishing, we went full speed most of the time. There were a few floating trees to contend with but not many.

As each stream or river entered our waterway, I asked them the name of it. They all had names and they knew them. I wrote down what they sounded like, Swanapana Agua, Papitcha, Tailin, Agulappas, etc. to name a few.

At 11:20, we saw a grand cayman—a small gator: he jumped off a log into the river. A large flock of birds circled like vultures but looked more like hawks or eagles, gray to white in color. At 11:30, we passed what looked like an old abandoned village, Toilin or possibly Aloepi. A small river flowed in from the left and we started drifting again. Up ahead I saw what looked like dogs swimming. When they saw us they snorted and took a dive. They were actually four otters; they stayed under until we passed. It is interesting to note that in taki-taki the otters are called "watra doggies". Two more fish were caught before the lead man hooked a big one as we came to boulder-strewn rapids: navigating the rapids was more important than the fish. At 12:00 we stopped for lunch, cassava and fish. They had a camp stove so no need to go after wood. While cooking, they caught two more fish, one was a small anjoemara.

We left at 1:25 and continued down the river. A large stream flowed in from the right, Culeajo. By 1:55 we came to our first large rapids. Before navigating the rapids, we had to land on the island located in the middle of the rapids and unload some of the supplies. The men worked the boat down the rapids—it was picked up and slid over the rocks and finally beached at the lower end of the island. The unloaded gear was hauled the length of the island and reloaded: by 3:00 we were back in the boat and on our way.

At 4:00 we stopped at an old camp used by the government geological department. Each one picked out a hut to use, settled in and made camp. The two younger guides started cooking, while the other three went fishing. On our side of the river, there were a lot of huge boulders. The water .rushing between the boulders made a beautiful spot to wash my clothes and take a bath. As the clothes were washed, I spread them on the boulders. Even after the sun set, the boulders were hot and kept the heat for a long time. Some of the clothes were completely dry: the first and only smoke-free dry clothes I had on this trip.

The fishermen came back with 10 or 12 more fish; so far they have not caught any piranha: they are in the river and no one goes in the water unnecessarily.

August 22
Bob's Birthday

The boys talked back and forth until about 1:00A M and were not too interested in moving at wake-up time. I started to push them and managed to get under way by 7:10. The weather had been very good and we needed to get moving to make Tepoe by noon and Paloemeu by 5:00 this evening.

At 7:20, we shot a good rapids—at 7:25, we missed the channel and hit a submerged boulder and slid off the boulder because of the heavy vegetation on it: a very exciting ride.

I noticed some macaws flying in their usual pair formation, always interesting to see. One was about three feet in back of the other and about three feet to one side. I guess the bachelors, maidens and widows/widowers fly single. They must mate for life. While in the jungle, because of the jungle canopy, I could not take a photo of them flying. Here on the river, there was a better chance: I tried but no luck. 7:32, more rapids; these boys are masters at this job.

At 7:45, I got out of the boat while the boys took it to the far side to work it through some rapids. Streams were still joining us from left and right and all happily add to the size of our highway.

Portage with flowers growing off the rocks

At 7:50, we came to an island where the river splits and falls off into deep and wide rapids. From my calculations, this was the Idenburghvallen Rapids. I was put ashore on the island with most of the supplies. The guides took the boat around to the shallow side and down to the lower end of the island. This island is a camp and a portage as well. The portage is about a half mile long. After the boat was secure, one of the guides took the bow and some arrows and looked for a fish that lives in these rapids; they called it a cumara.

We were not the first to portage here. This island had a standard setup for portage. Years before, someone built a log road the length of the island; if needed, the boat can be dragged the length of the island.

While waiting at the lower end of the island, I noticed that all the boulders under the fast running water had heavy vegetation growing on them. The plants were of very coarse fiber which made for excellent footing—they were blooming at the time. The flower stem was about six inches tall: the lower three inches were under the fast flowing water and the three inch tall pink blossoms were above the water. I took a few photos of the flowers: one had a bee visiting it.

Closeup of the portage flowers

Two days before, on the way upriver, the guides offset a 55 gallon drum of gasoline and some motor oil. The gasoline was now divided up into some smaller portable gas tanks for our continued trip. The supplies were moved from the upper end of the island and loaded back into the boat along with the 55 gallon drum. We left at 9:00 but with no extra fish.

We continued on at a good speed and came to some small rapids which we were able to navigate. We stopped and went ashore to shoot some monkeys: three big ones, one a mother with a baby. The baby hung onto its dead mother. If we tried to take it from her, it started to cry so we let it be. On the river again there were more rapids to shoot and streams still coming in to join the river. At 9:50 we came to rapids which were a bit rough in passing. We stopped at a sandy beach to clean out the spark plugs: we departed at 10:10.

At 10:20 a small river flowed in from the left. The guides wanted to stop and eat but I said no; they could eat when we got to Tepoe: we moved on.

At 11:00 we came to rapids which were big and rough by my standards. According to my calculations, this would be the Lothvallen Rapids. The boys got ready to do their jobs: get into the proper slot then shoot two square turns on boulders with little more room between than the length of the boat. A lot of this is done with the motor in reverse. The two men in the bow, one with a pole the other with the paddle, were ready. Timing was the most important element. One goof and it's finished. We made the first square corner but the bow hit about two feet too high on the next boulder and would not slide downstream. The stern was pushed against the rocks, the boat rolled over and we took on water.

A half day from the end, disaster strikes. I had a special canvas bag to carry my camera, notebook and first aid kit. When approaching rapids everything went into the bag and it was made secure. As the boat went over, my first thought was for this bag. I could lose everything else but not that. The skipper had detached the motor and the fuel tank and was standing on a boulder holding them—I can't imaging how he got there with the motor so fast. The men were pulling everything out of the boat and passing them up to a boulder. Everything got wet and a lot of things went down the rapids. One of the younger men was at the bottom of the rapids grabbing things as they came.

Damn near drowned—quite exciting. We lost one monkey, the one with the baby, and one of my boots, which was later recovered, but I was still alive and had my bag.

At 11:40, we came to another island with big rapids. I got out and walked to the end of the island. Everyone else got out too because it took everyone outside the boat to guide it through the rapids. We were off again at 12:10 and ran into more rapids shortly: these were short but good. At 12:30 we saw our first people since starting on this river journey. They were in small boats fishing. Later we stopped for a short time at a Suralco camp. We were then off to Tepoe with no more problems. We arrived there at 1:00.

Boys have a contest to see who can throw a rock across the river

There was a couple from Holland living and working there. He was a Doctor and as quite usual with the Dutch, he spoke very good English. While the guides went about their business, I talked with the Dr. and his wife. I enjoyed two glasses of good juice. I told them of my trip and some of the encounters along the way. They told me one of their projects was studying parasites. From my travels, I learned that the Indians go into the streams or rivers to defecate. The couple said this practice made it difficult for them to get samples for studies. However, at night the people in the village went out into the jungle, away from the village, to defecate. So the couple went out at night with a flashlight trying to locate samples to test in the lab for parasites. Needless to say, the Indians were sure they were nuts.

While in Tepoe, I called Neil Bittle on the short wave radio and told him I had arrived at Tepoe and was proceeding on to Paloemeu.

We departed about 2:30 with two extra passengers, the boat captain's, wife Pataowa, and their baby. There were no rapids between Tepoe and Paloemeu so we were going full speed all the way. We arrived at Paloemeu by 6:00. I went to the runway and the "control tower" and radioed Zorg-en-Hoop that I had arrived at Paloemeu and everything was OK—Kelly could pick me up tomorrow.

There was a large building between the runway and the river where transients could stay. It was built so hammocks could be strung crossways the length of the building. This was like a pole barn—we hung up our hammocks and called it a day. Piesolie his wife and baby were in one hammock—a family size one.

Pisi had a special paddle which I convinced him to sell to me—another memento of this exceptional trip.

Captain Piesolie; his wife, Pataowa; the crew lookout; and me, standing where the Paloemeu river empties into the Tapanahoni

VIII

Back Home and After

August 23

This morning Kelly arrived in the 182 for the trip back home. Two of my sons, Rory and Bob, were on this part of the trip. My supplies and other items along with the parrot I had picked up in Alalapadu were loaded. The flight was uneventful and we were back at Zorg en Hoop in no time.

Ma was waiting with the van. My first memory of my return was Camille saying that **"you stink from smoke".** For sure I must have smelled from smoke like the Indians—I had been to a different world and back.

It took some time to settle in with the kids asking questions all at once. First of all, it was necessary to get the smoky clothes off and take a good shower. Next item—wash the clothes.

I unpacked all of the goodies I acquired on the River Trip and we had a show and tell. The little green parrot was introduced to Flint, our macaw, he let us know of his disapproval. I spent the last week of my vacation just resting.

One of the first things I discovered during this time of my vacation was some extra problems with my feet. I went to see Dr. Brocksma to have him check them out. After looking at them he went for a book. After a while he started to laugh and handed me the book. It was in English, so I read what he pointed out: evidently some parasite had invaded the sores in my feet. The Dr. explained that these were little bugs that live on dogs and had somehow gotten into the open sores in my feet. The book said: "No known cure". These bugs tunnel under the skin looking for a home. Dr. said that they could not live in humans but burrowed for a while looking for a home—finally they die. To speed their life's journey, he recommended the use of a Freeze spray. These critters made upheavals in my skin in the feet like a ground mole. Wherever they traveled, the skin was upset and turned somewhat red. By freezing the area, we hoped to shorten their life expectancy.

Now, if one were to like some excitement, try to freeze a part of your foot, like the arch—now that feels - different - . Eventually the bugs were either frozen or just died for lack of food—eventually my feet returned to normal.

All the items I purchased at Alalapadu had been delivered by MAF—we now sent the money to cover my "line of credit" to Alalapadu by way of MAF.

The local newspaper had followed my journey.—after my return, I called the Editor and told him I was safely home. The trip was great and left 20 pounds of my weight in the jungle—I didn't keep it off very long.

Was the trip worth the time and effort? It sure was and a lot more too. Over the years, I marvel at how small our basic needs are—we can live on very little and most of our needs are at hand. The people I had lived with had only the basics and that was all we needed. My trip with these Indians gave me a new philosophy. While we search for more of everything, we already have more than we need.

Prior to their conversion, the Indians had a great fear of everything. With Christ, they lost that fear. They know that with Christ they are safe. One of the advantages of the trip was seeing how these Indians enjoyed this new found Faith. They may lose some of that early glow later but I witnessed that glow when I was with them. They sang songs and prayed because they found joy in it. It was not a job to do—it was something they found fulfilling. A better title for this book might have been "A journey to my Roots".

Shortly after my return, I spoke with the Suralco General Manager, Waldo Porter and invited him and his wife to come to the house and view the slides taken on the trip. They did and we all enjoyed the evening.

Later we moved to Paranam, closer to the Suralco operations, where the jungle is close by. When I heard the howler monkeys start to howl at night, I would step outside the house just to enjoy listening to this hauntingly beautiful symphony.

A reminder of

A Journey into Another World.

Supplies

- 24 lbs dry rice
- 10 lbs dry red beans
- 10 lbs dry white beans
- 4 small packs of hard candy
- 1 lb salt
- 18 chicken broth cubes
- 44 beef broth cubes
- 3 ½ oz jar minced onions, dehydrated
- 3 real lemon juice
- 4 - 3 ½ oz. tea packs
- 1 box tea bags (20)
- 2 lbs coffee
- 1000 gram can Quaker oats
- 4 small cans Nestle condensed milk with sugar
- 3 boxes 16 ga. shotgun shells 1 buckshot - 2 No. 2
- 1 - 2 cell flash light
- 2 extra batteries
- 1 extra bulb
- 1 gas cigarette lighter
- 4 extra gas cartridges
- 9 extra lighter flints
- First Aid Kit - snake bite kit, adhesive tape, gauze, cotton, band aids

- Iodine, sulfa ointment, cotton swabs, tooth picks, 2 tubes of the farine, 4 - 100 tablets aspirin, constipation pills, diarrhea medicine, 2 phenergan cream(insect bites), malaria tablets, Vitamins, Vaseline.
- 1, 6/12 insect spray
- 200 ft. ¼ "nylon line
- Compass
- 6 contour maps
- 1 lb Sevin
- 2 lbs kalk
- Asahi Pentax 35mm camera
- 5 rolls 36 exposure Ectachrome
- 2 pants, 2 shirts shorts, T shirt, 3 sox, sun glasses, tooth brush, tooth paste, razor, shaving cream, mirror all of this in a small plastic bag.
- Moetete
- Small bag for camera and film
- Buck hunting knife
- Machete with case
- Jungle hammock
- Light blanket
- Jungle boots
- 2 enamel dishes
- 2 enamel cups
- 2 plastic spoons
- 2 plastic forks
- 2 plastic glasses
- 1 small aluminum tea kettle
- 2 aluminum pans with covers, 1-16", 1-22"
- 1 small alcohol stove with (Braund spirits)
- Army web belt with canteen
- 1 water bag
- Fishing gear, nylon line, sinkers, bobbers, steel leader and large hooks
- Toilet paper

Lightning Source UK Ltd.
Milton Keynes UK
UKOW040110140613

212209UK00001B/261/P